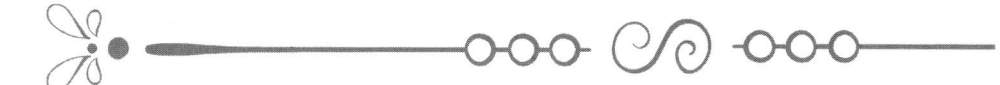

Happy Birthday

Guests

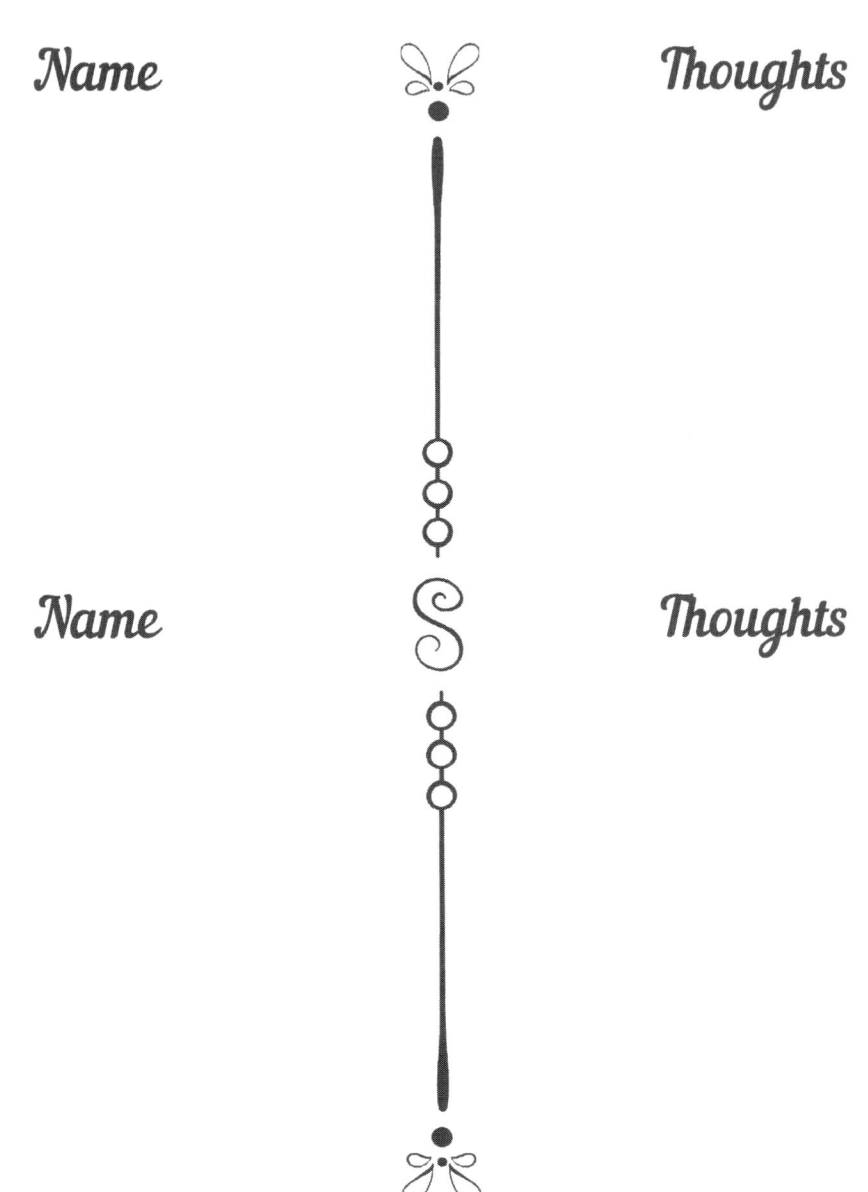

Name   Thoughts

Name   Thoughts

Guests

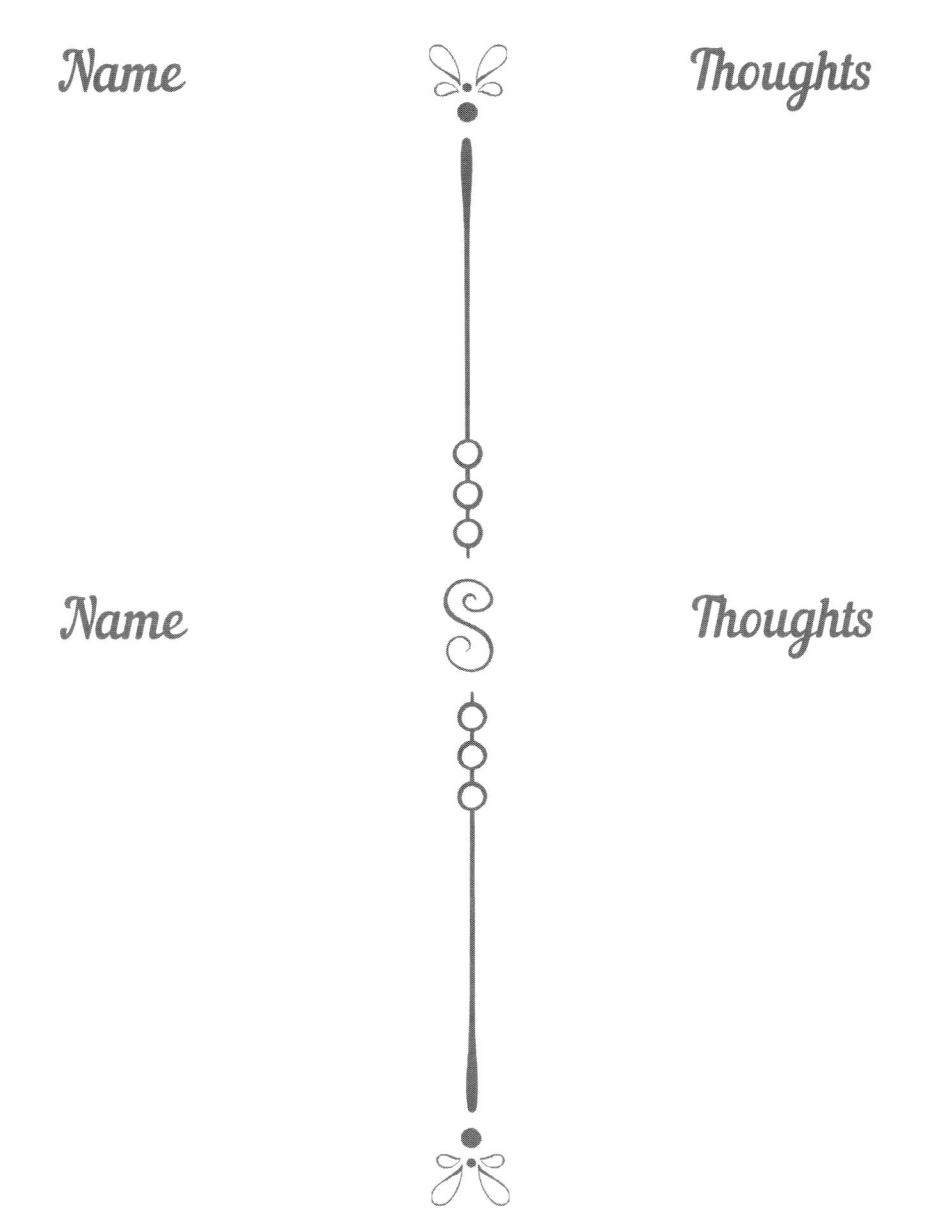

Name · Thoughts

Name · Thoughts

Guests

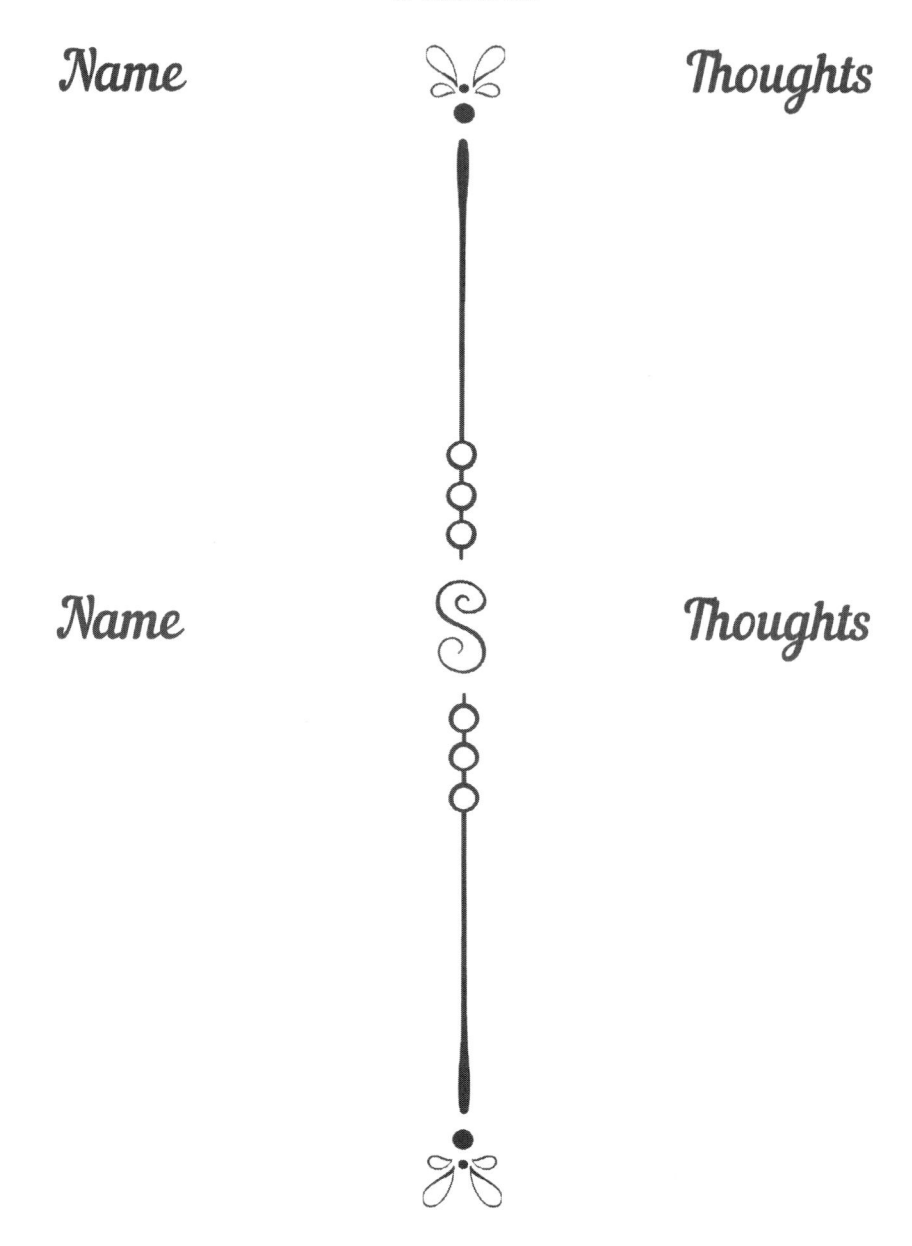

Name *Thoughts*

Name *Thoughts*

Guests

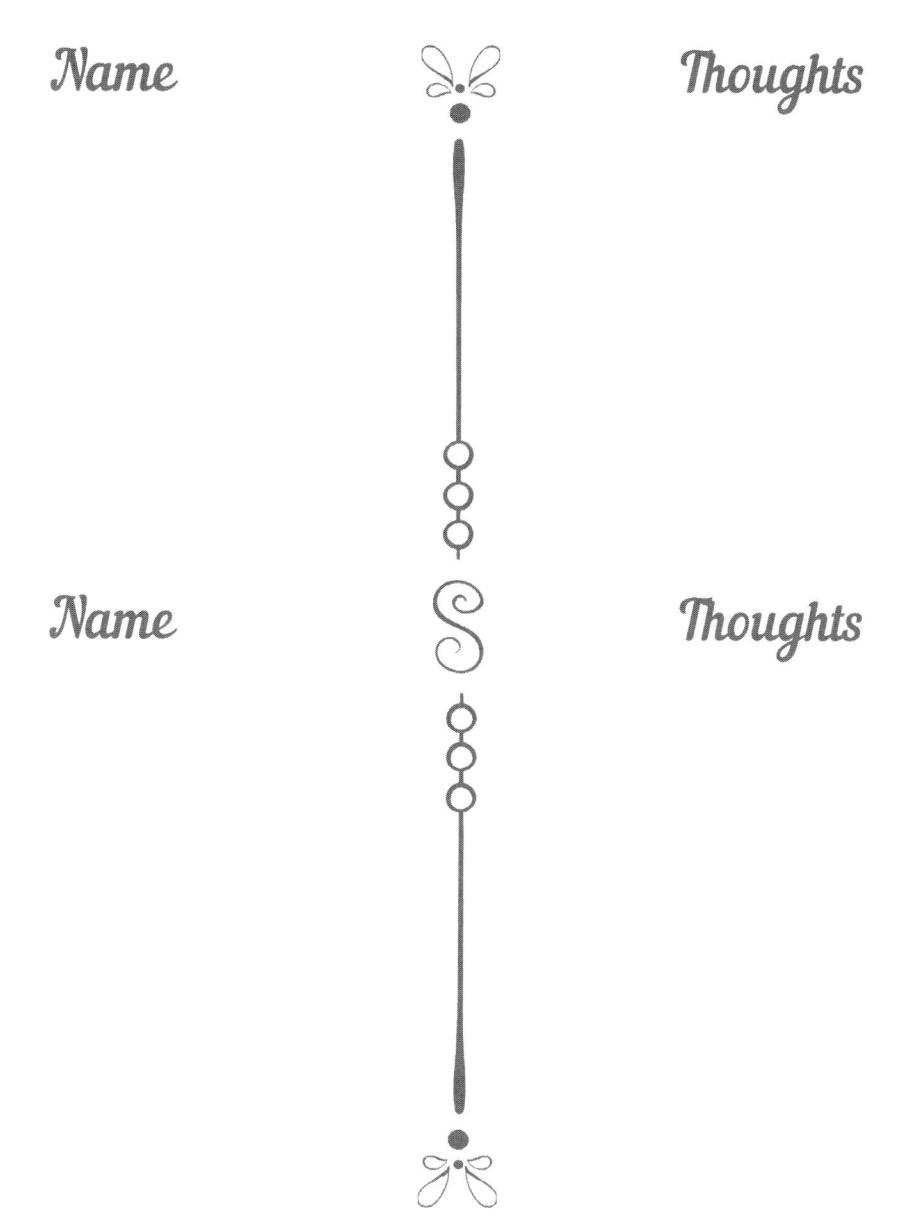

Name　　　　　　　　　　Thoughts

Name　　　　　　　　　　Thoughts

Guests

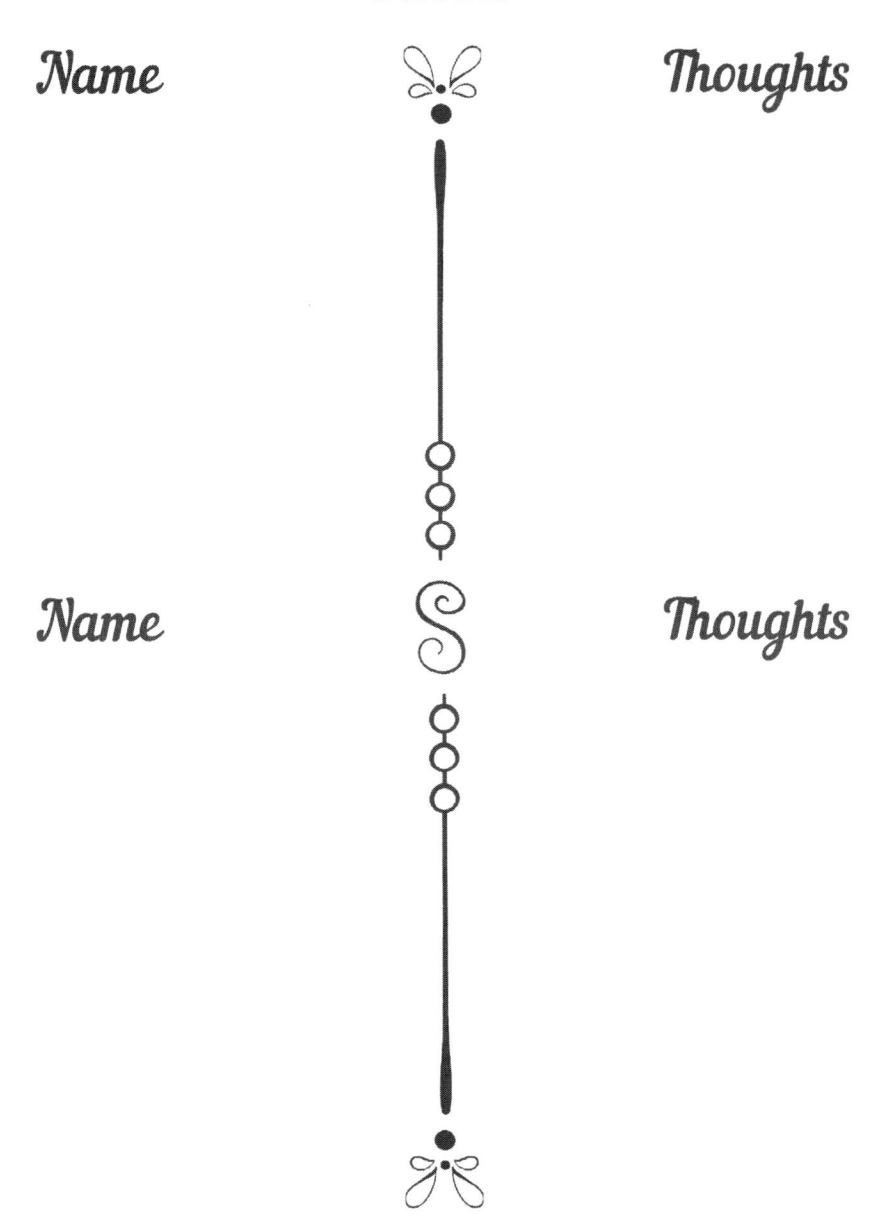

Name Thoughts

Name Thoughts

Guests

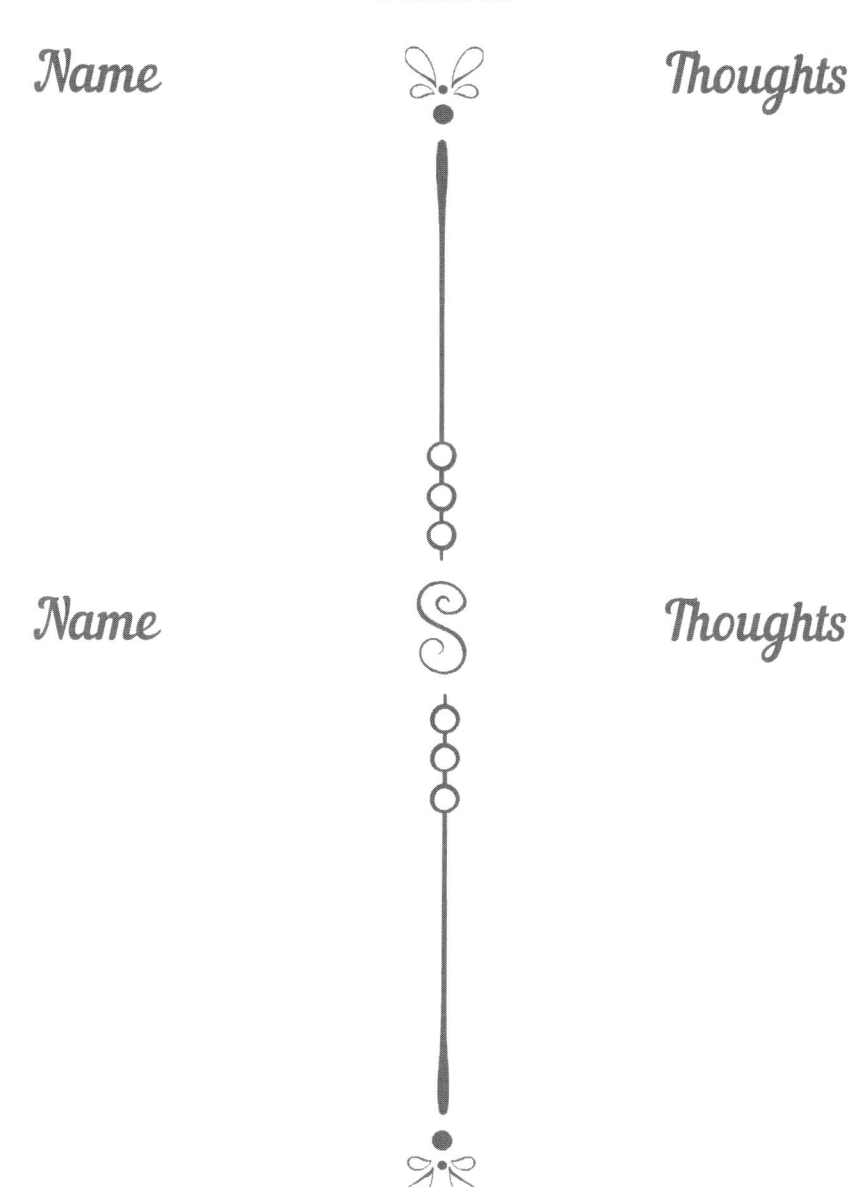

Name　　　　　　　　　　Thoughts

Name　　　　　　　　　　Thoughts

Guests

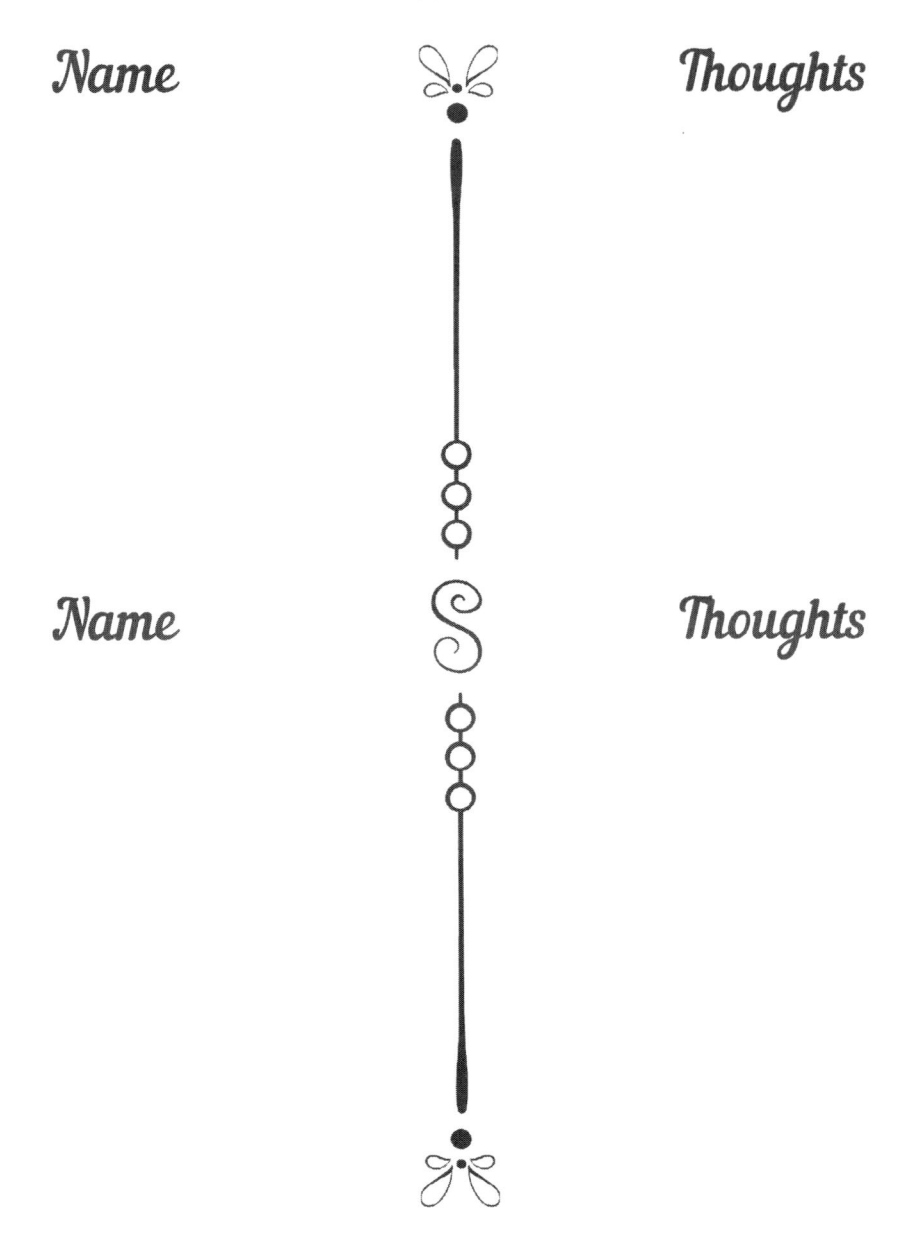

Name Thoughts

Name Thoughts

Guests

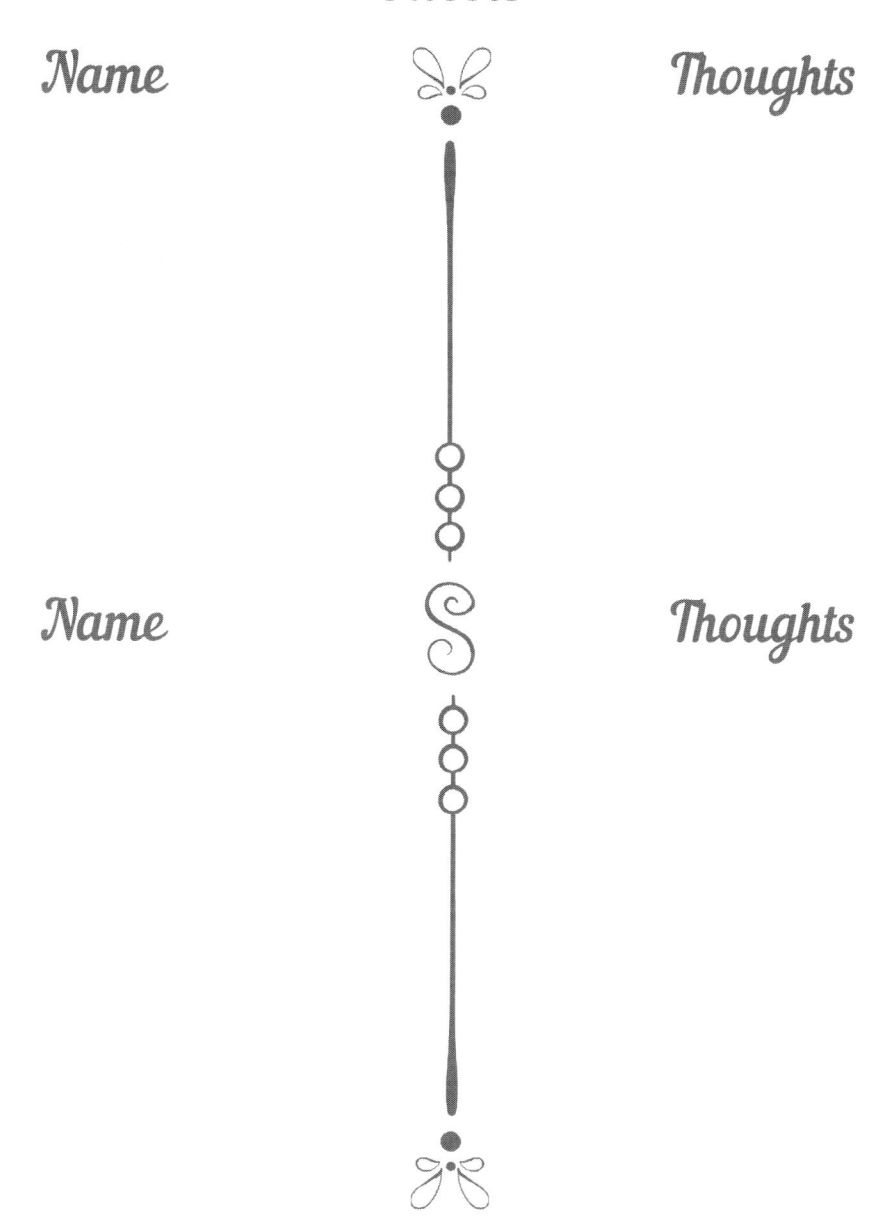

Name	Thoughts
Name	Thoughts

Guests

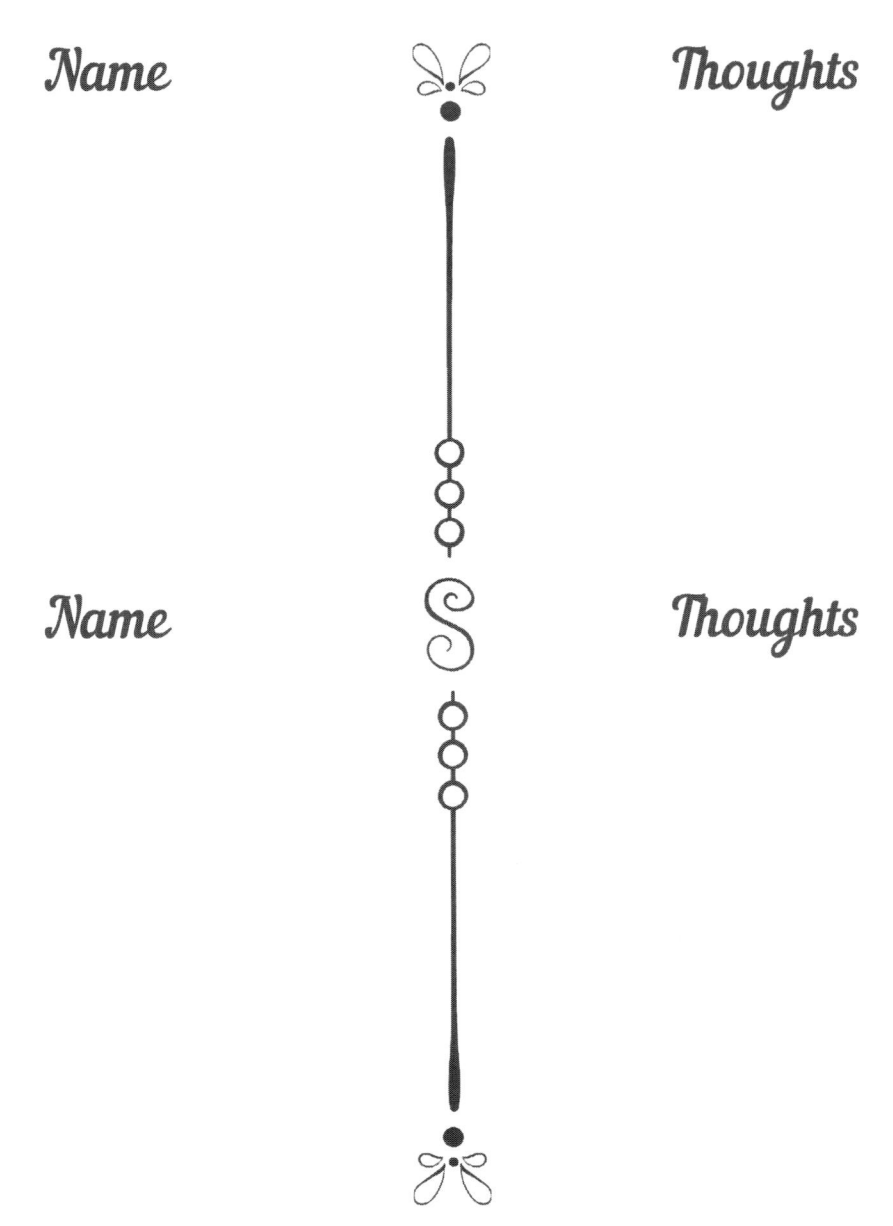

Name　　　　　　　　　　Thoughts

Name　　　　　　　　　　Thoughts

Guests

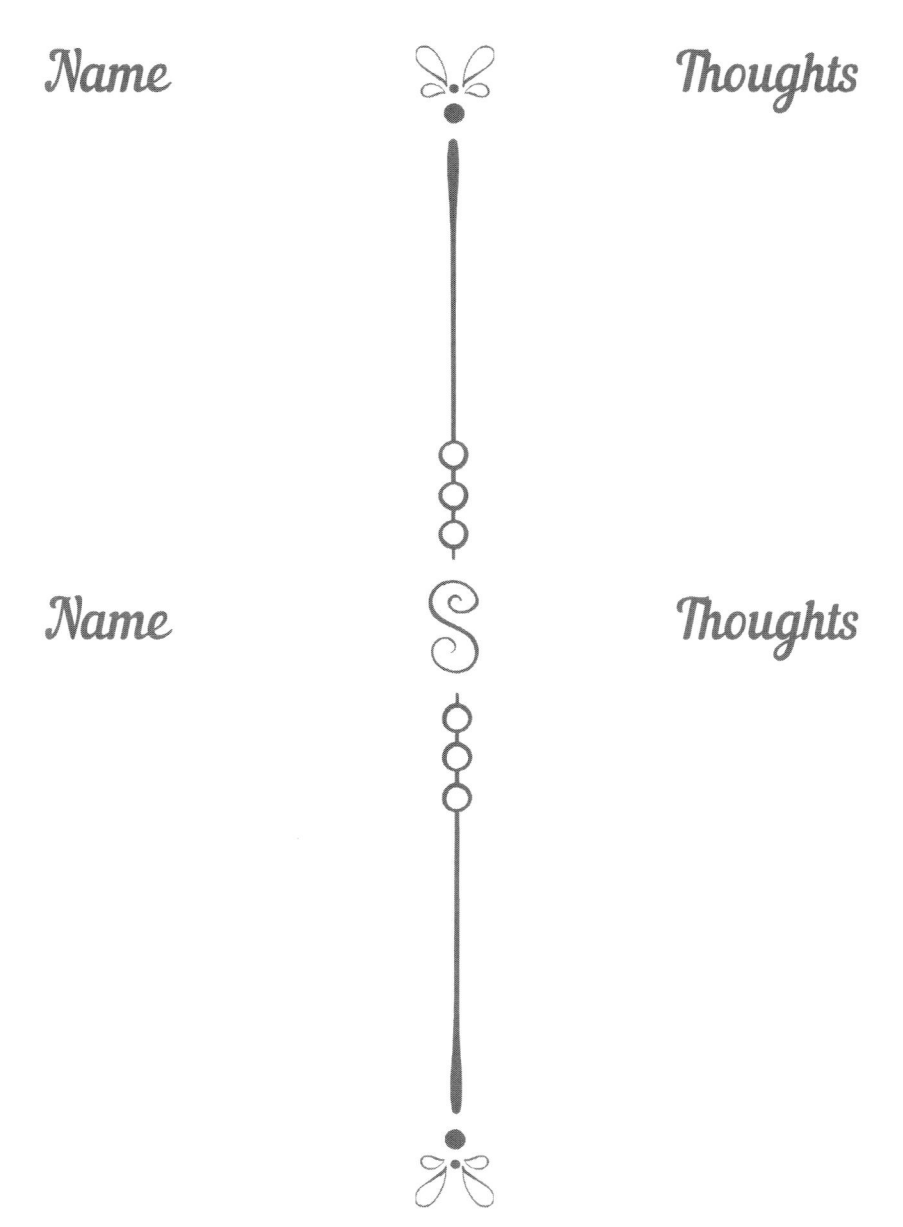

Name   Thoughts

Name   Thoughts

Guests

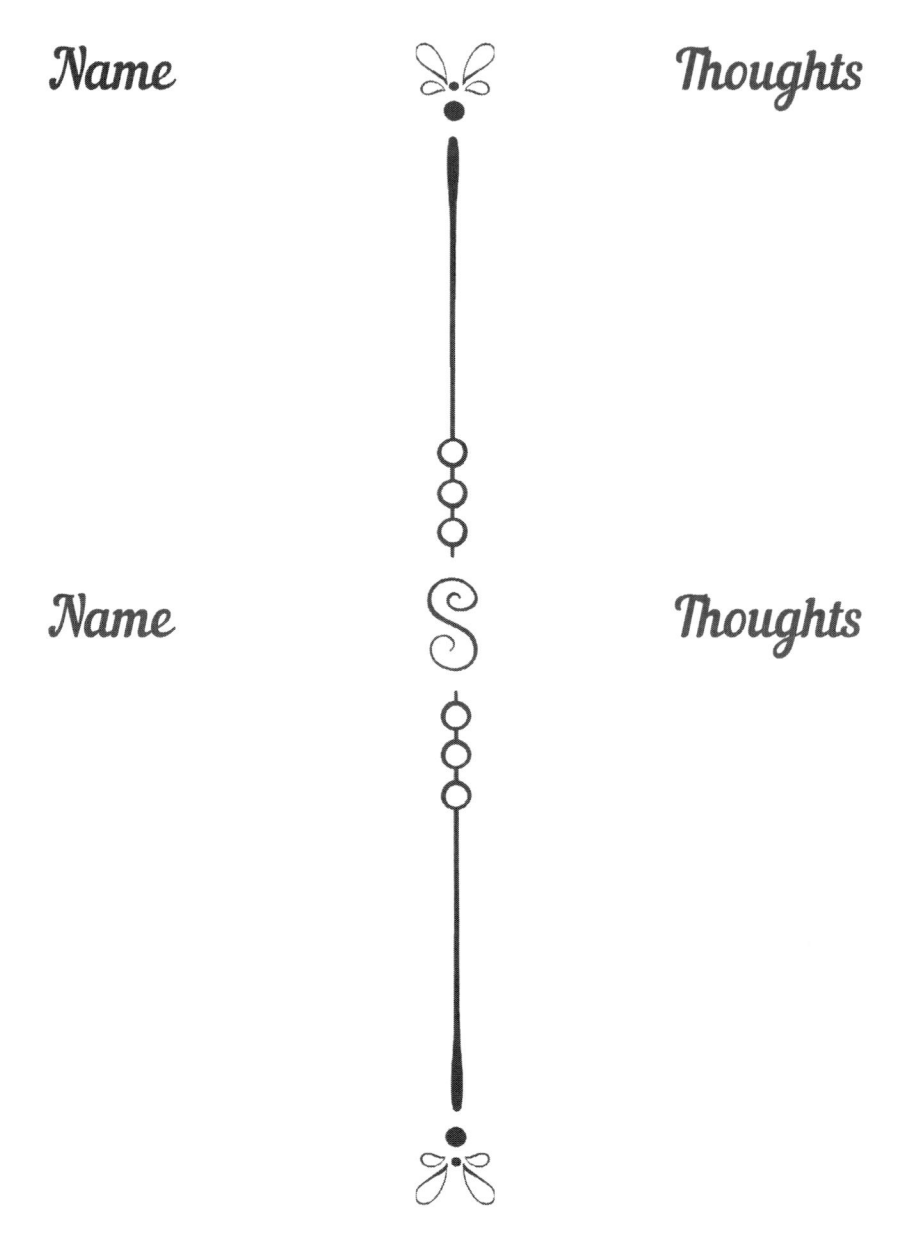

Name　　　　　*Thoughts*

Name　　　　　*Thoughts*

Guests

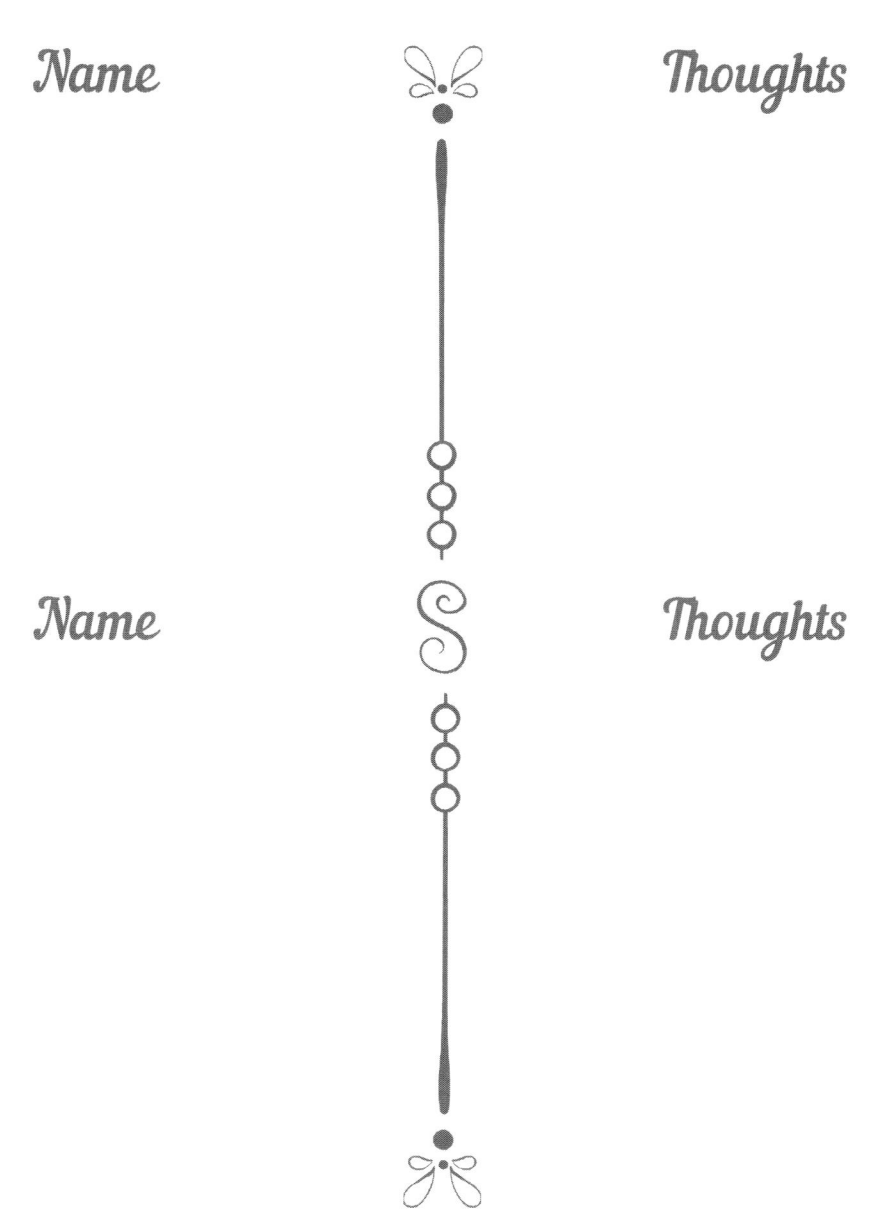

Name — Thoughts

Name — Thoughts

Guests

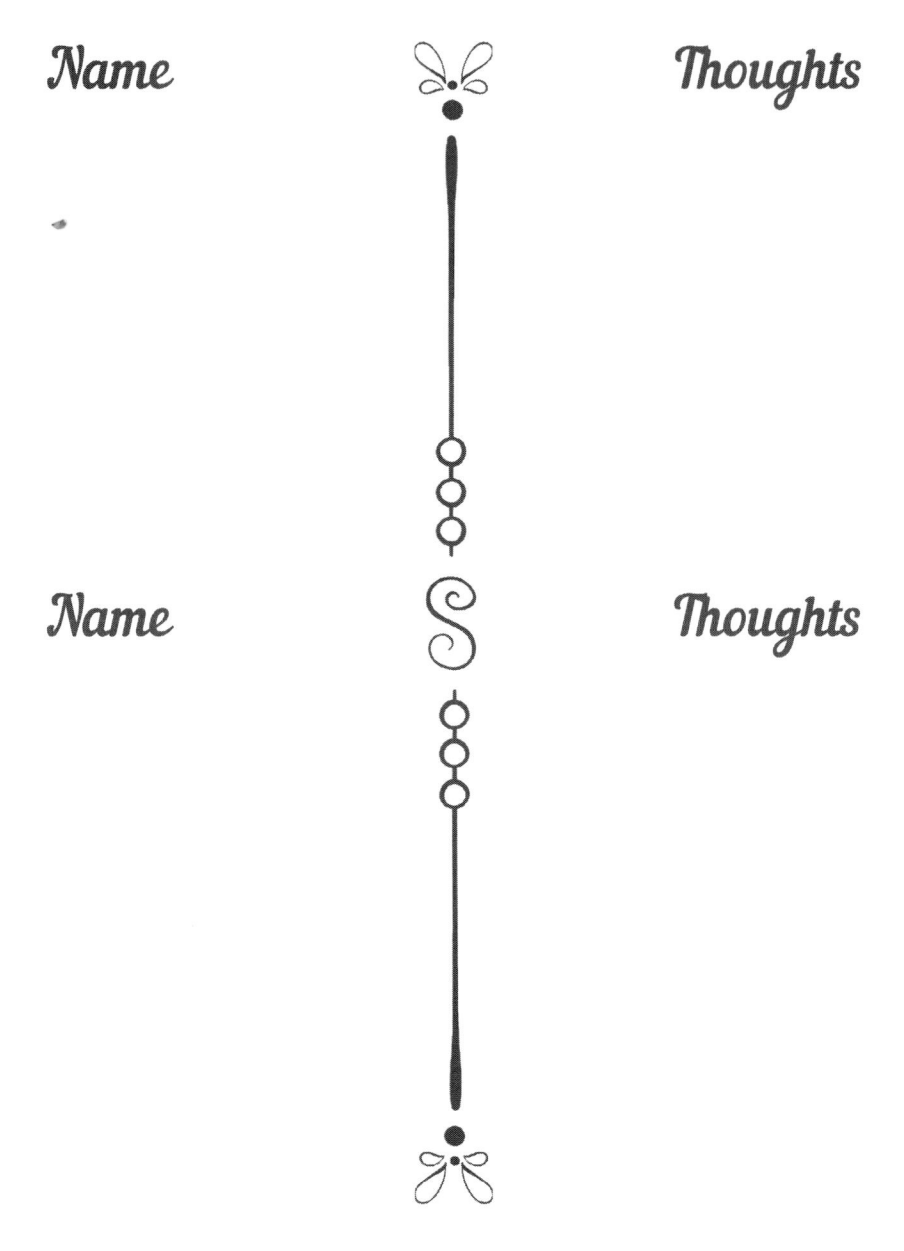

Name   *Thoughts*

Name   *Thoughts*

Guests

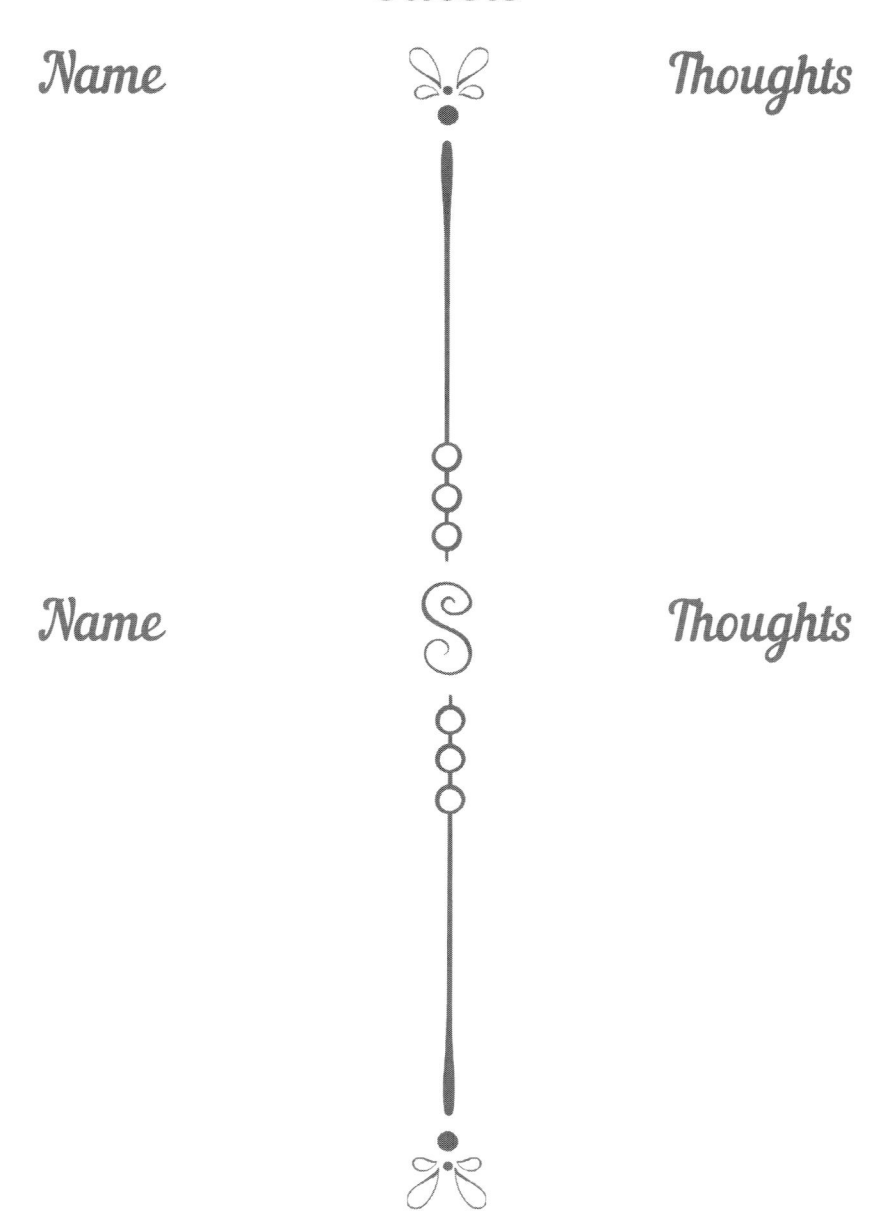

Name · Thoughts

Name · Thoughts

Guests

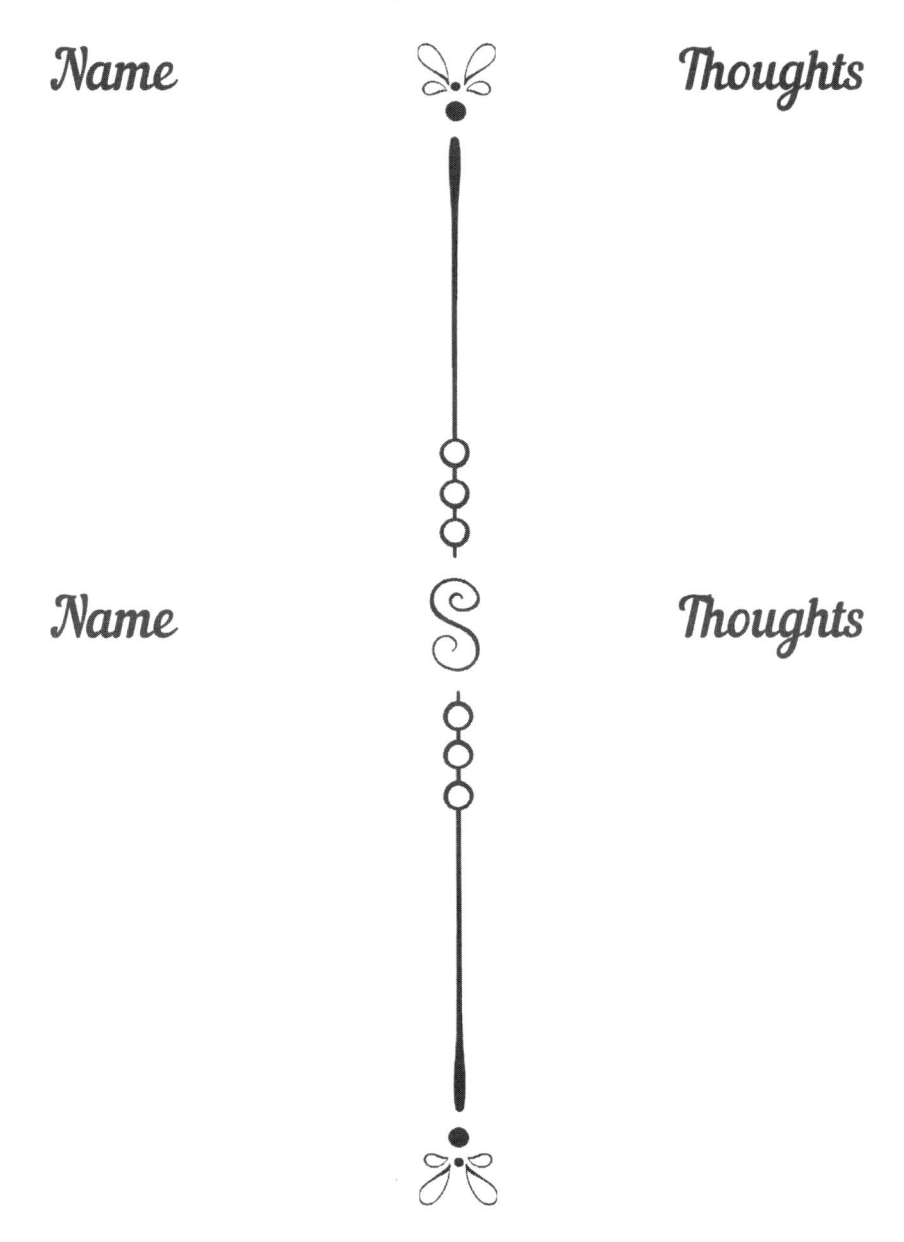

Name   *Thoughts*

Name   *Thoughts*

Guests

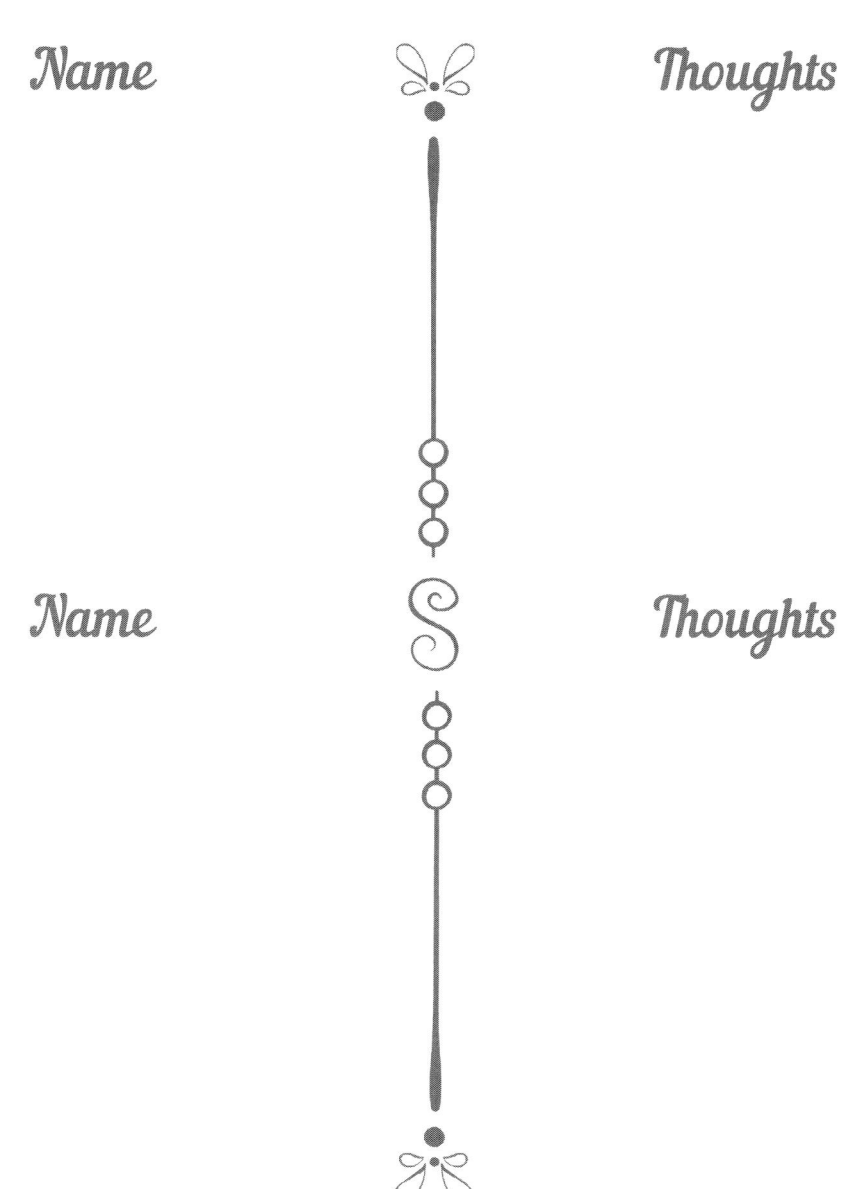

Name · Thoughts

Name · Thoughts

Guests

Name　　　　　　　　　　Thoughts

Name　　　　　　　　　　Thoughts

Guests

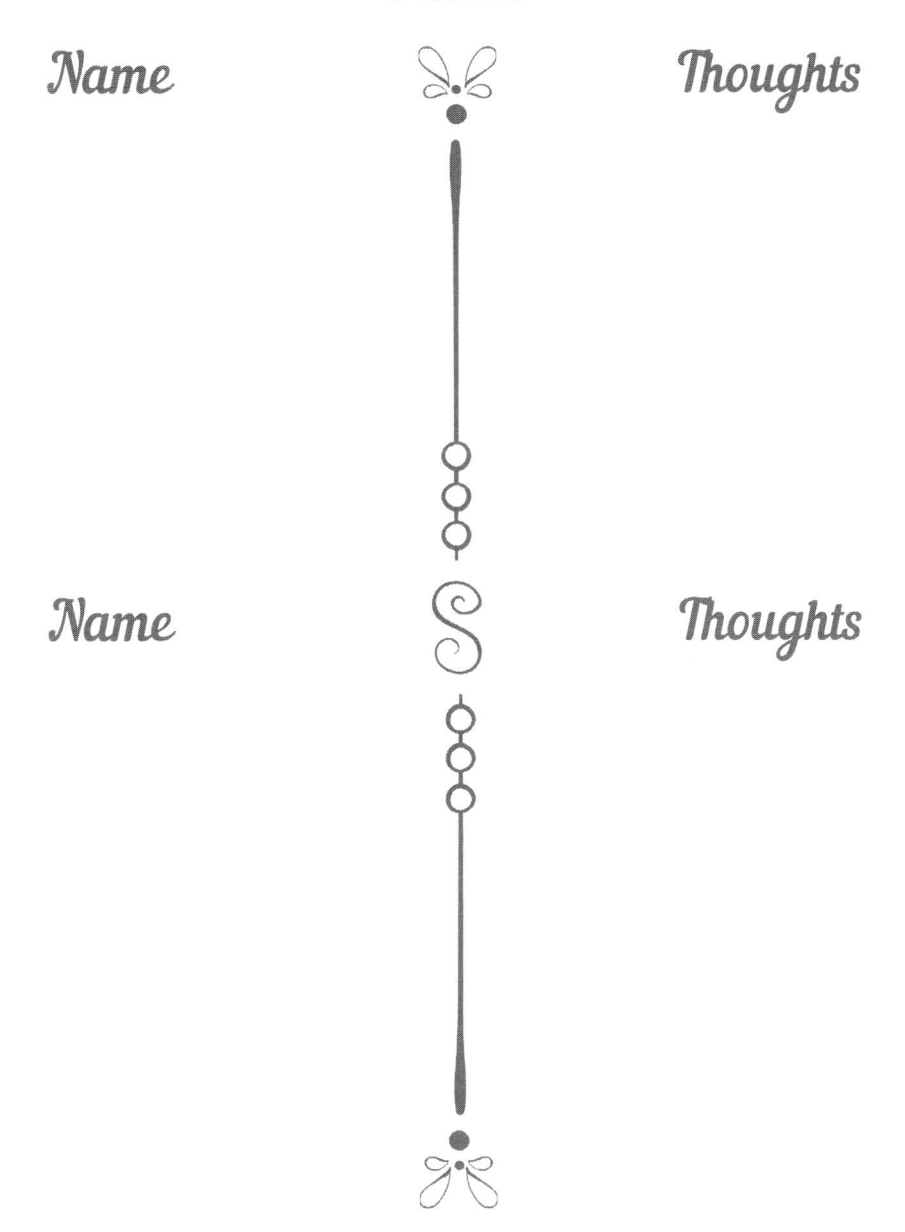

Name   Thoughts

Name   Thoughts

Guests

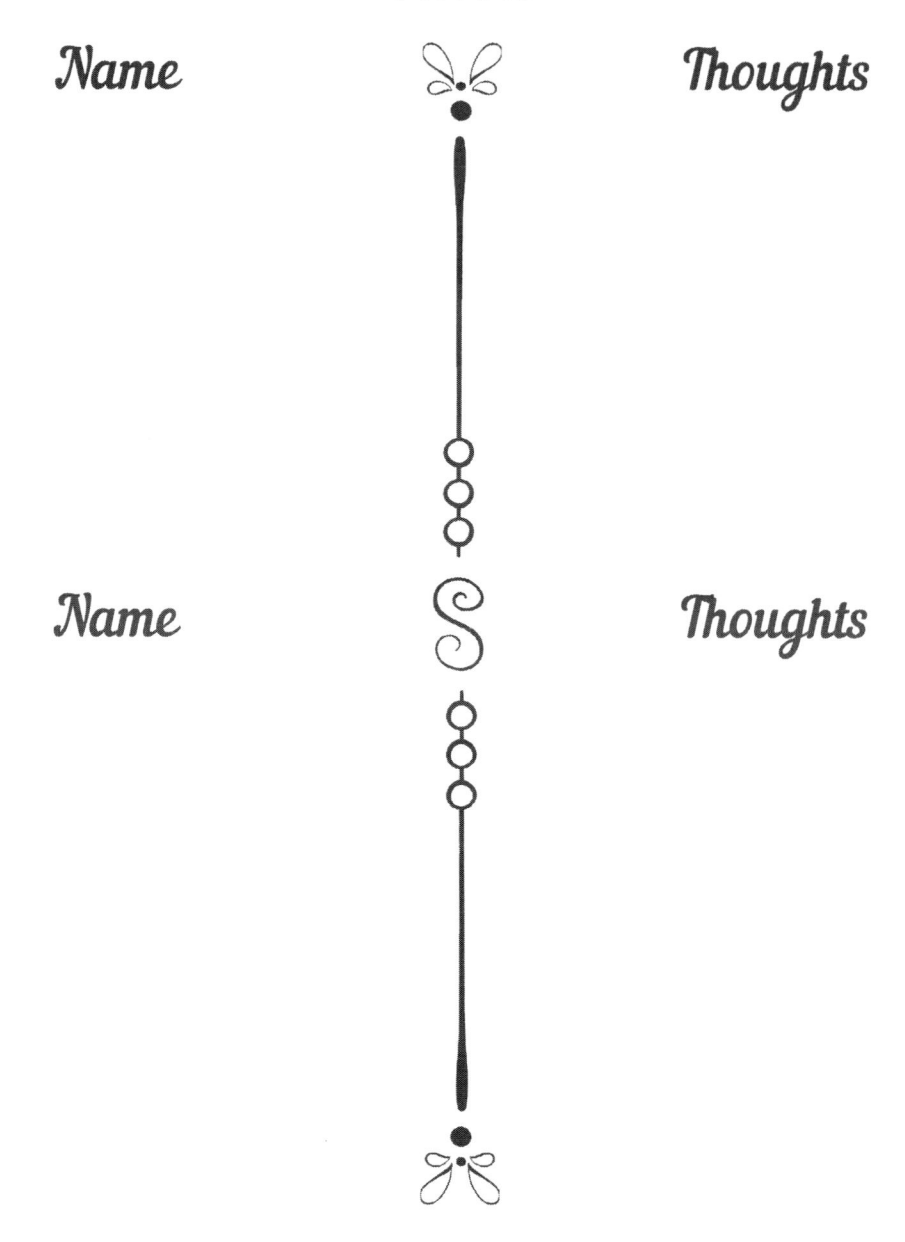

Name   Thoughts

Name   Thoughts

Guests

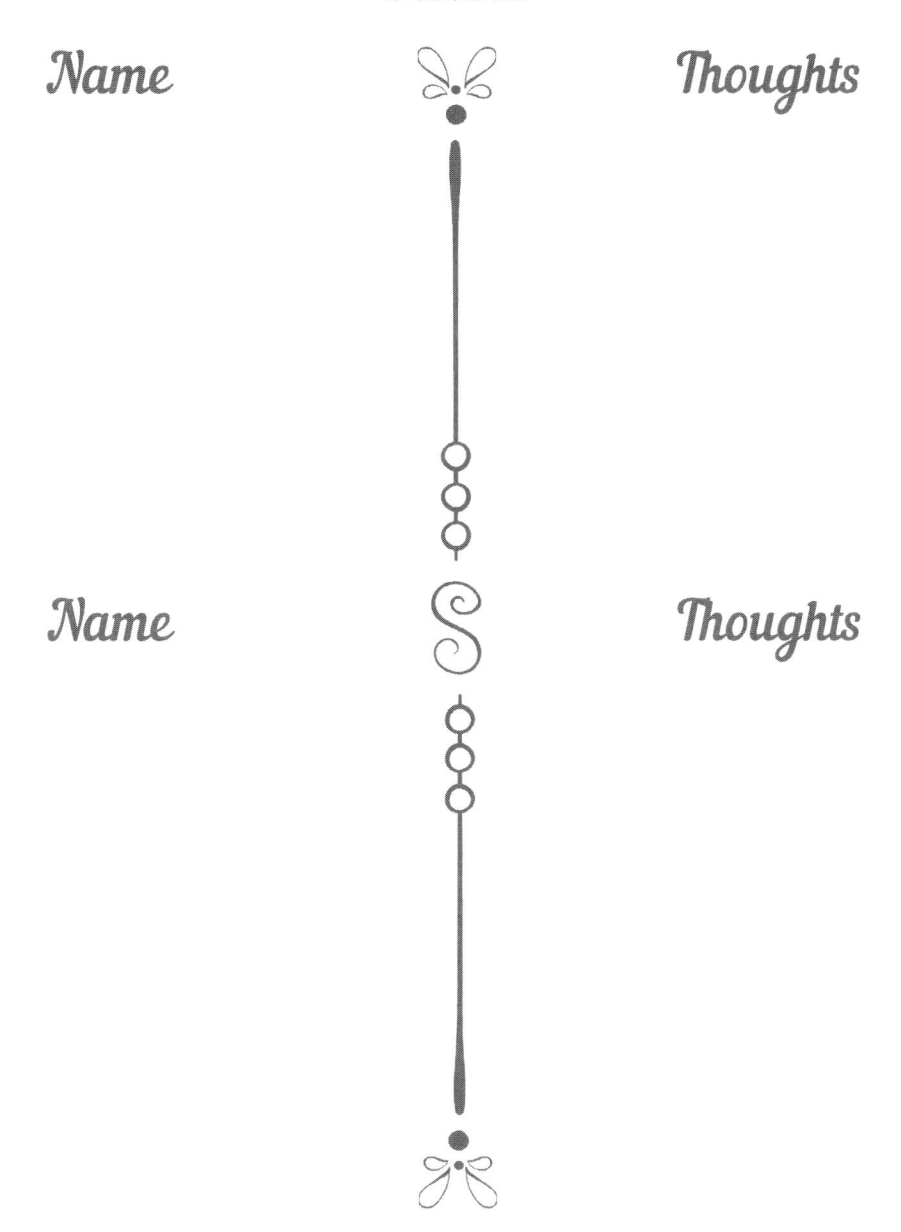

Name　　　　　　　　　　Thoughts

Name　　　　　　　　　　Thoughts

Guests

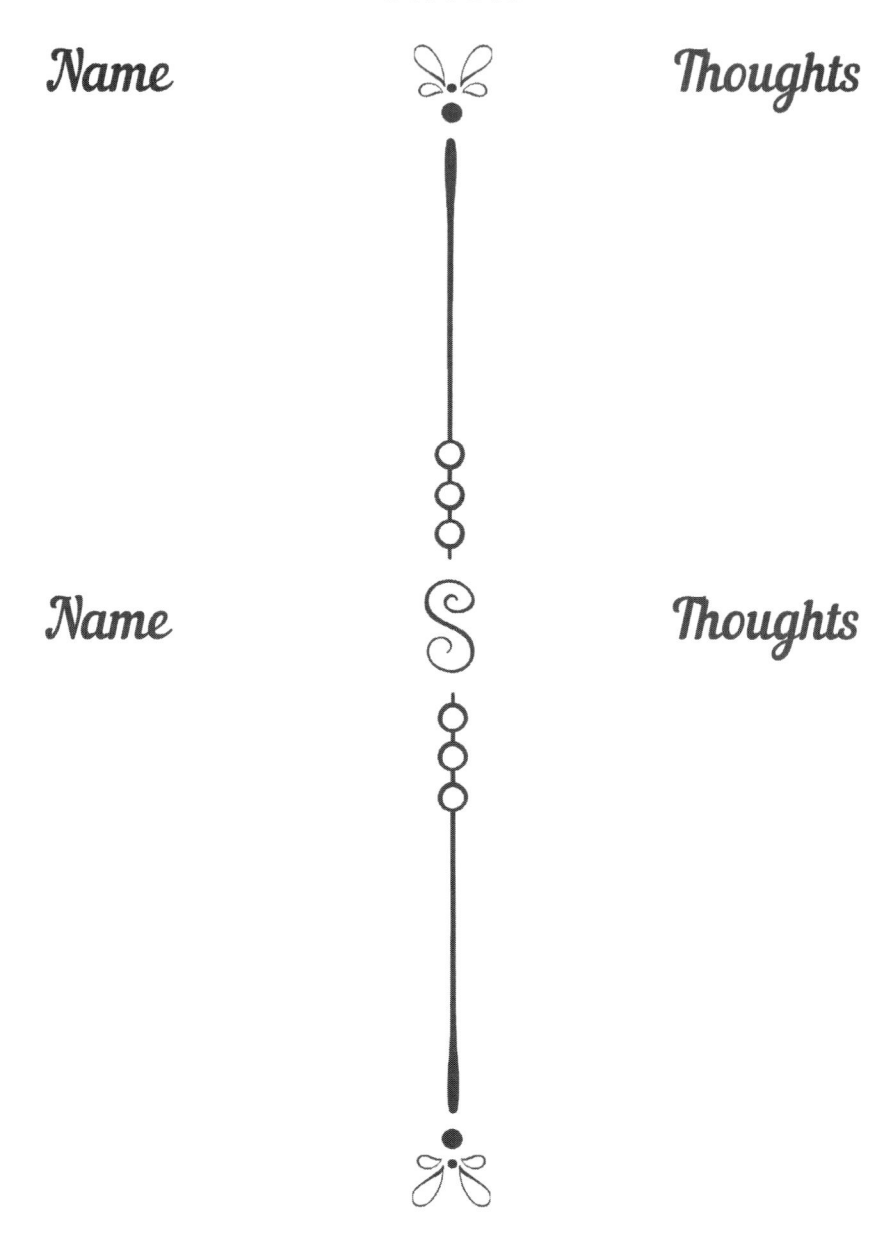

Name   *Thoughts*

Name   *Thoughts*

Guests

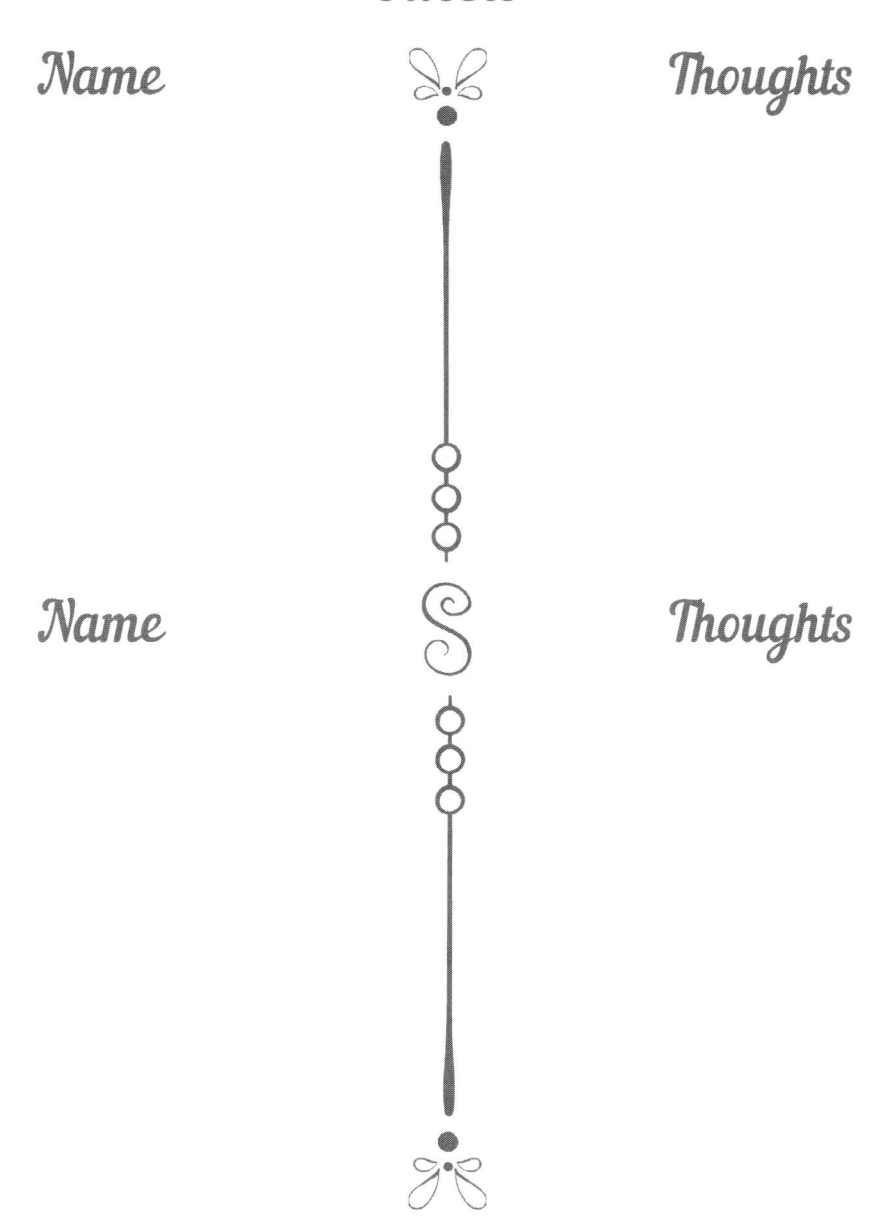

Name   Thoughts

Name   Thoughts

Guests

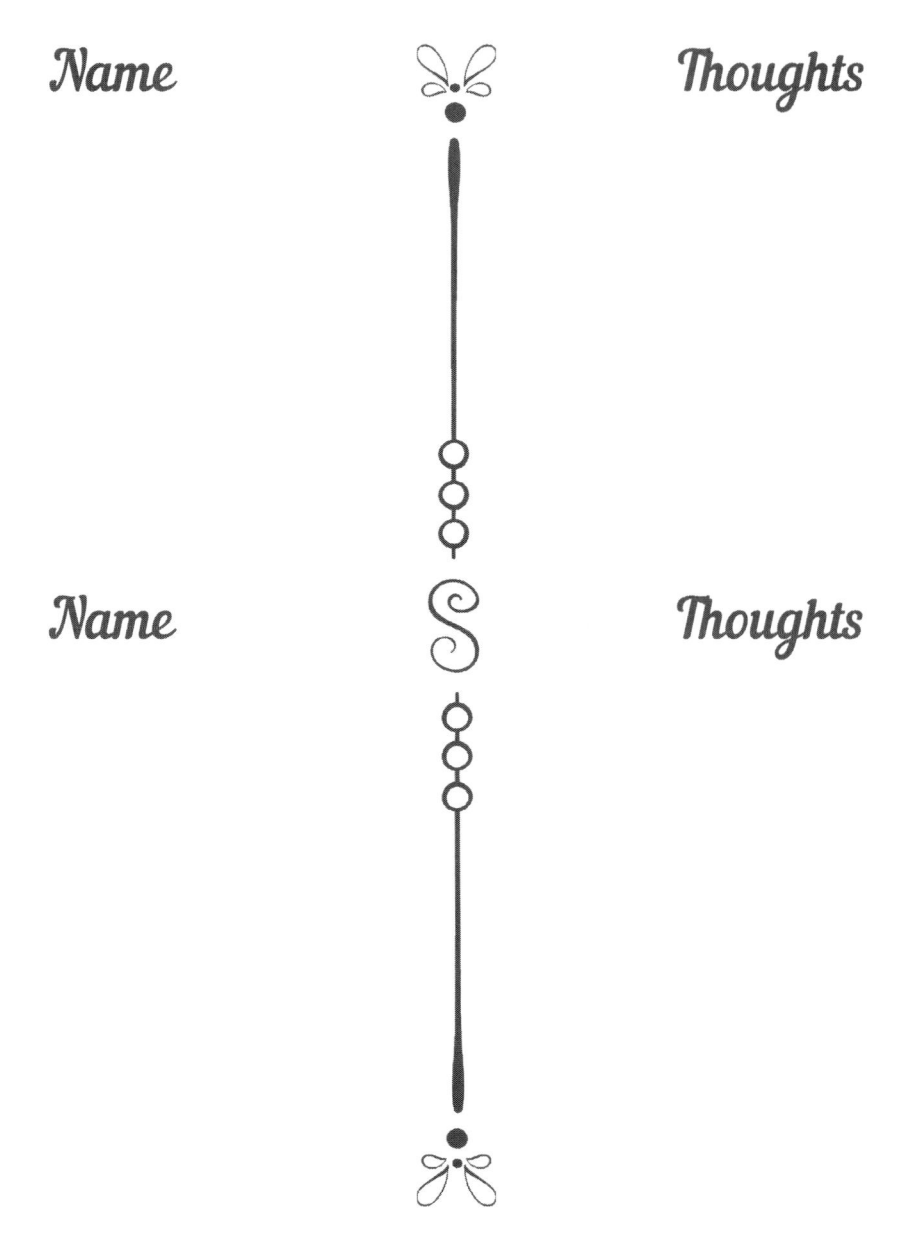

Name · Thoughts

Name · Thoughts

Guests

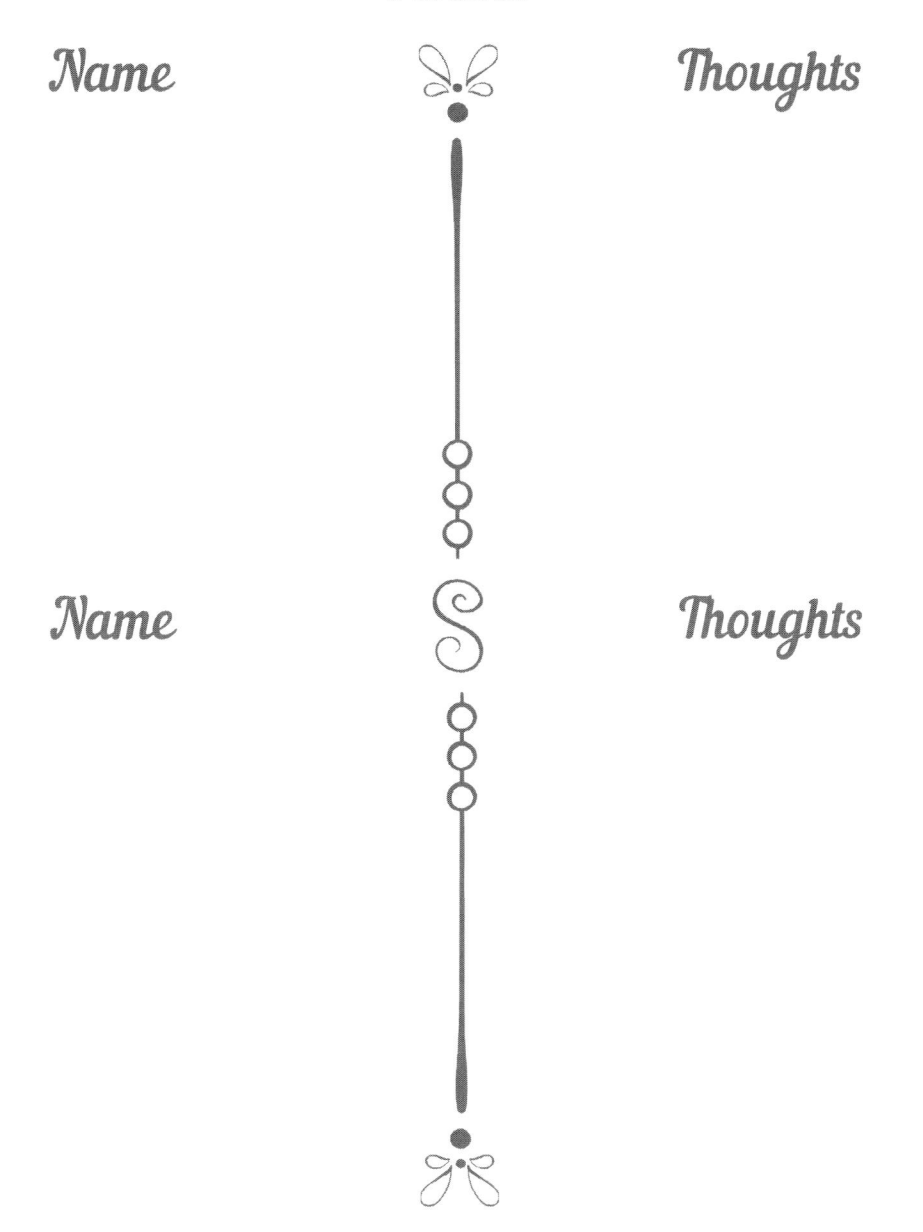

Name   Thoughts

Name   Thoughts

Guests

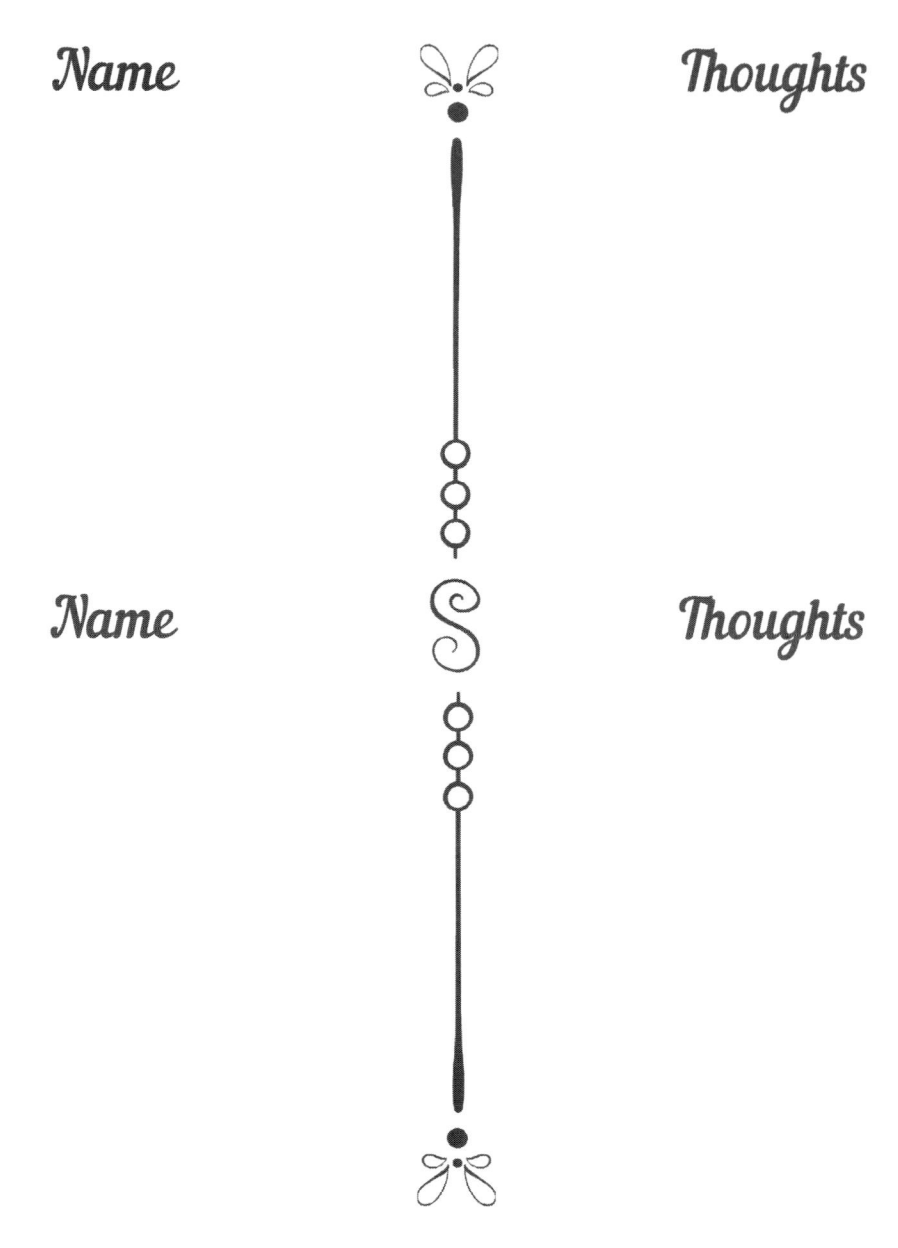

Name   Thoughts

Name   Thoughts

Guests

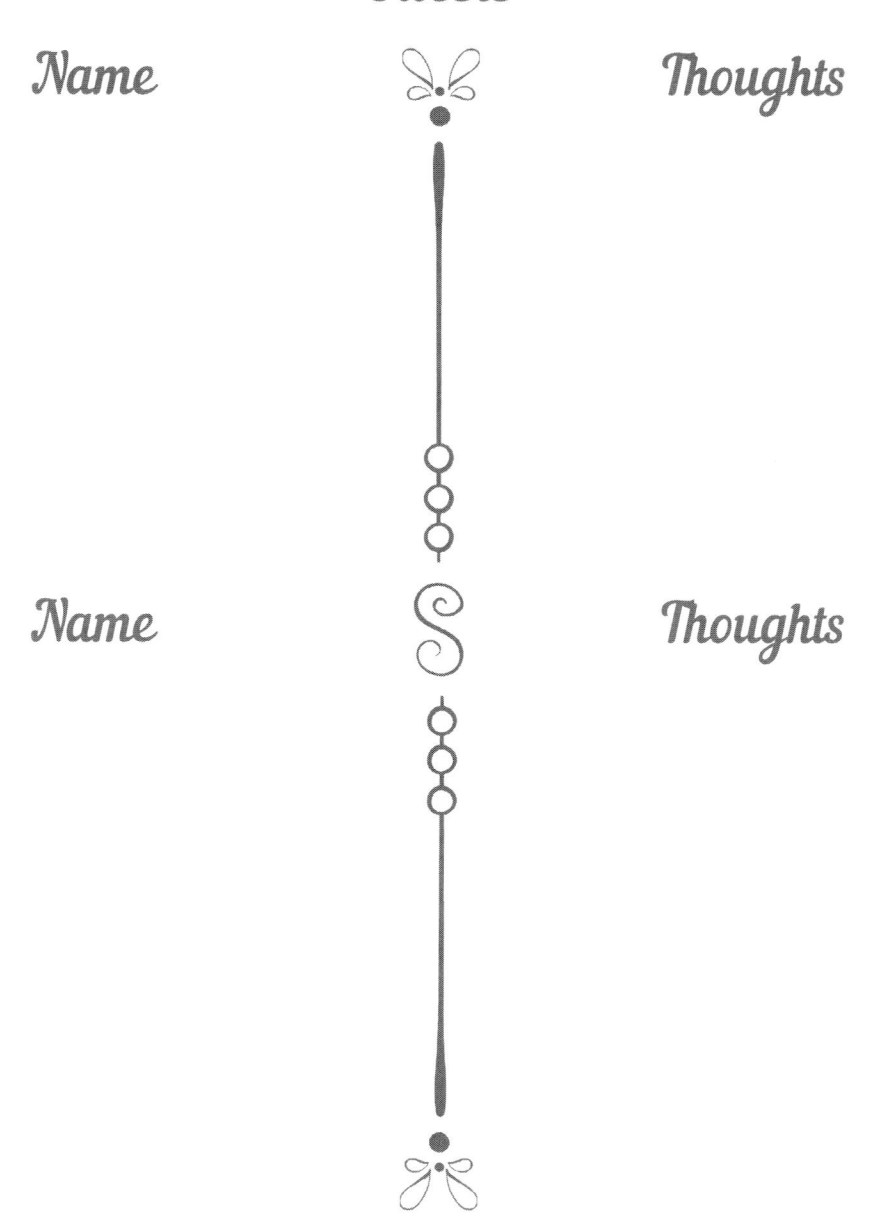

Name · Thoughts

Name · Thoughts

Guests

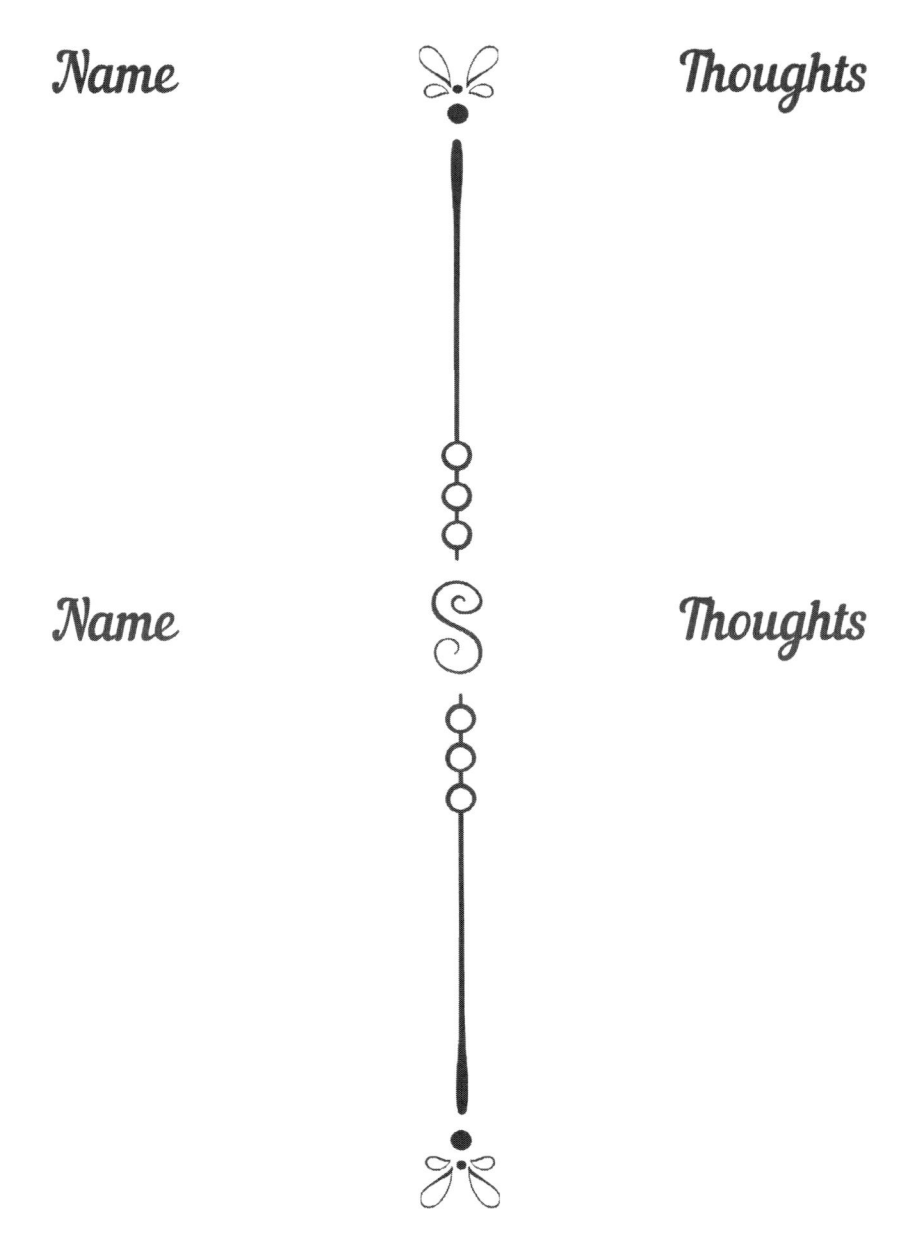

Name **Thoughts**

Name **Thoughts**

Guests

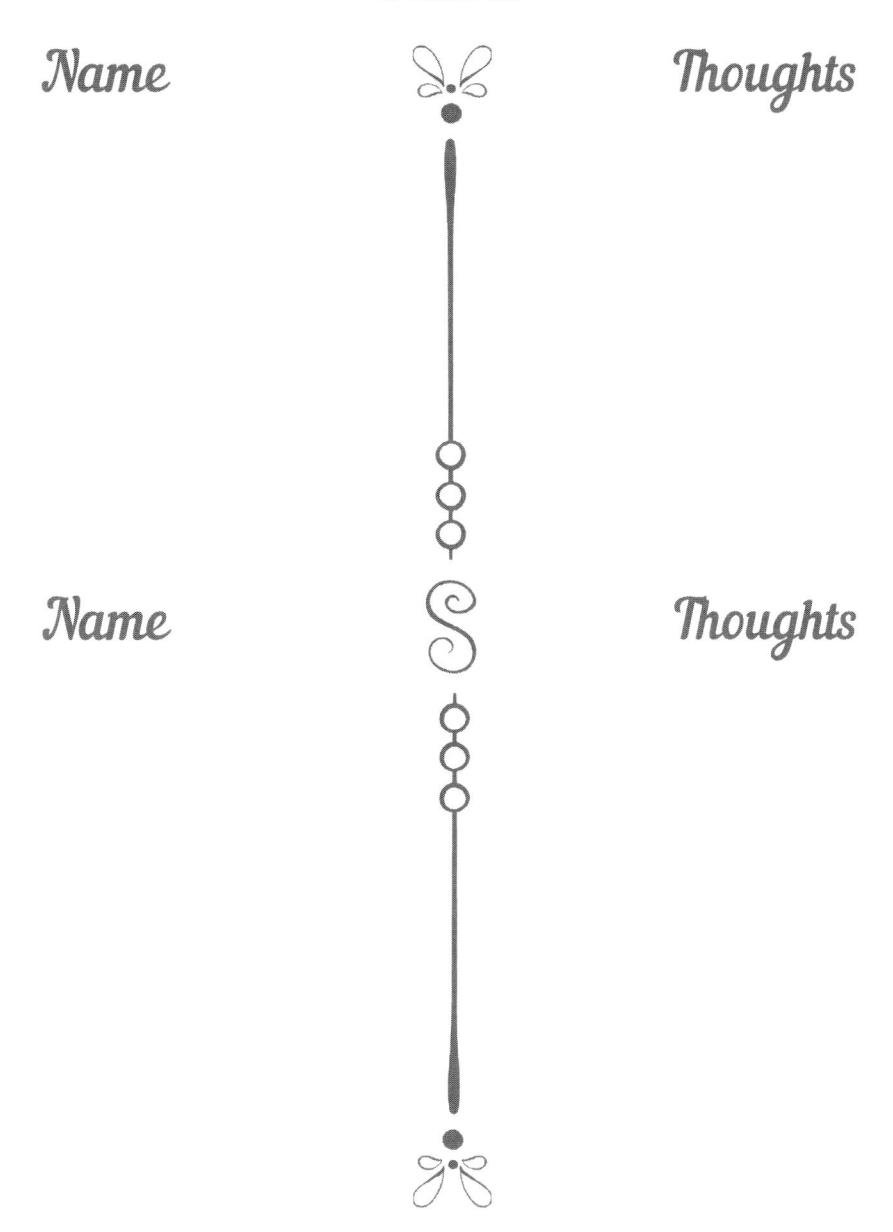

Name | Thoughts

Name | Thoughts

Guests

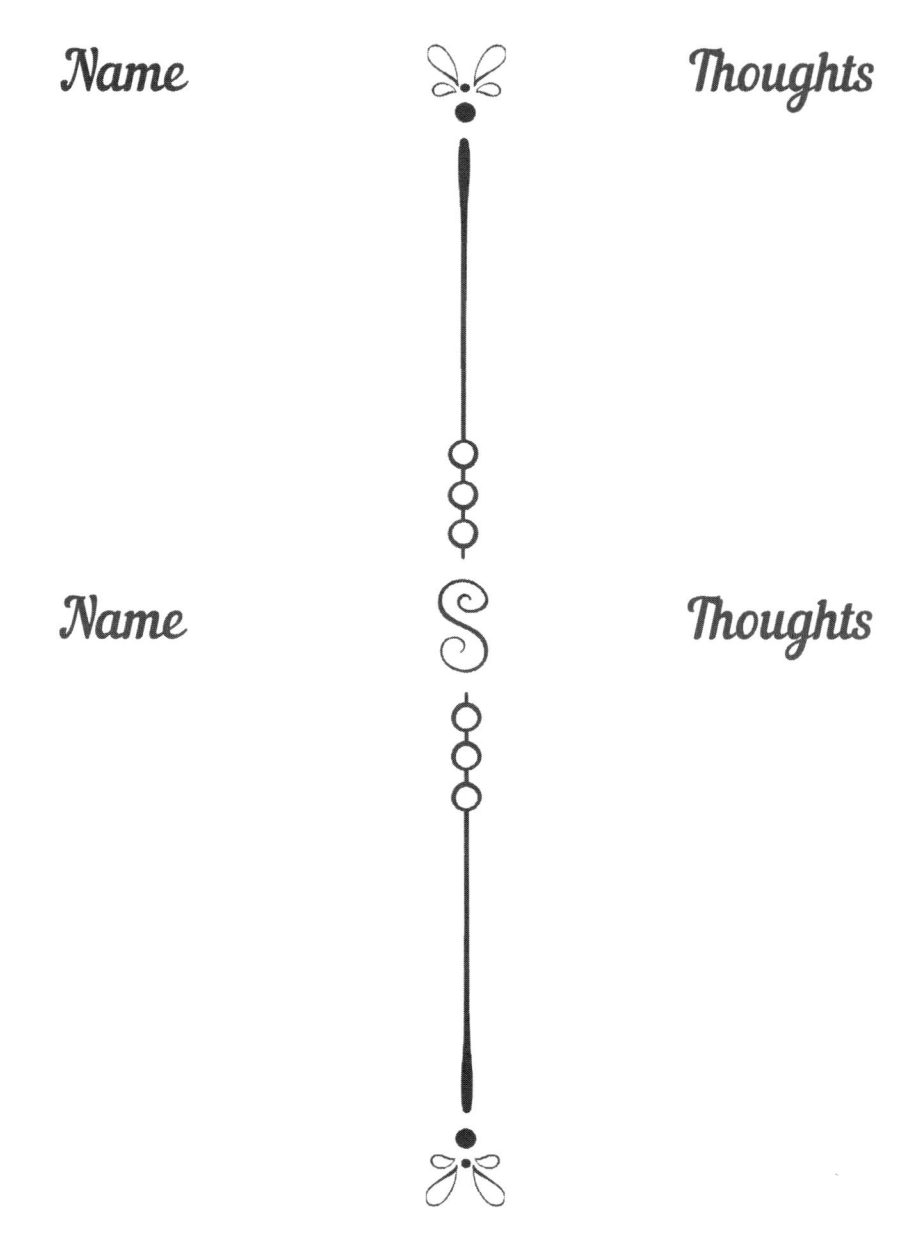

Name　　　　　　　　　　　Thoughts

Name　　　　　　　　　　　Thoughts

Guests

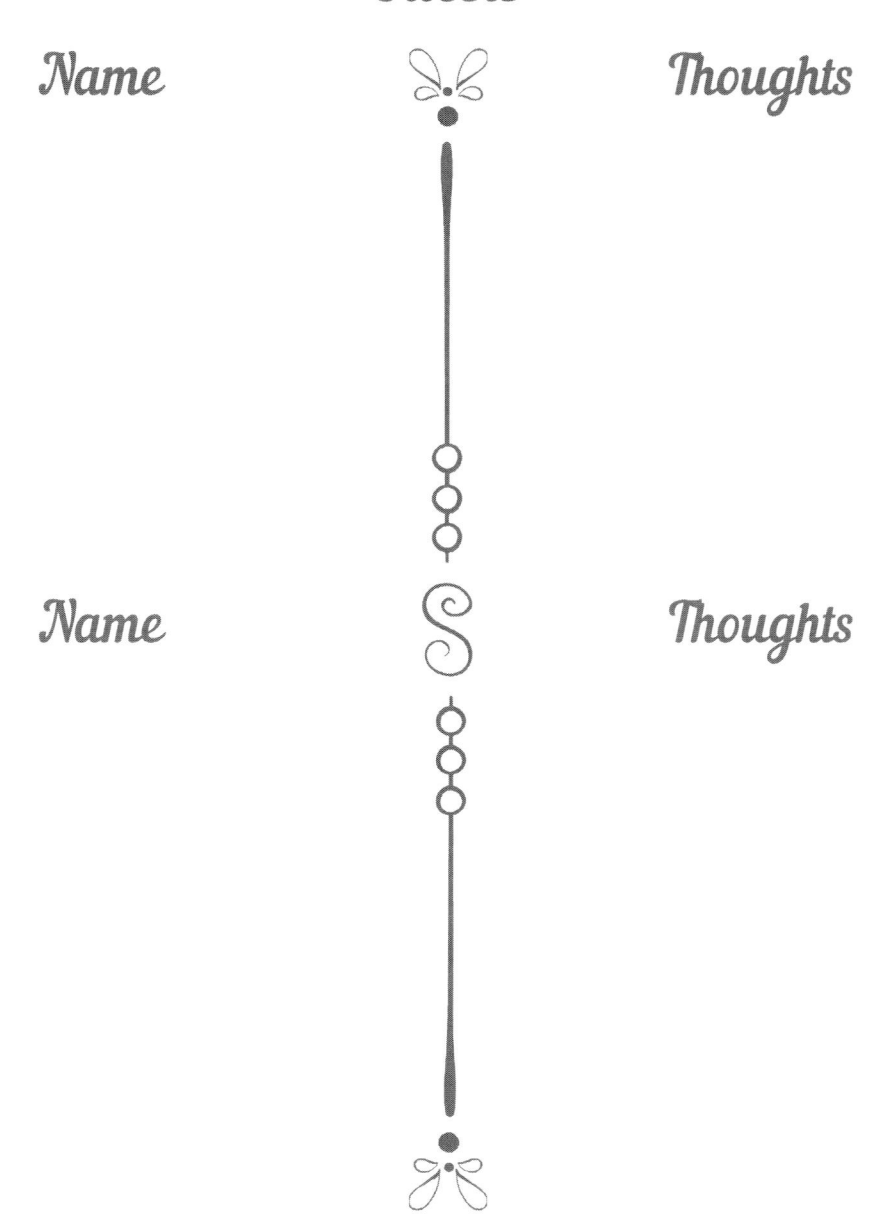

Name · Thoughts

Name · Thoughts

Guests

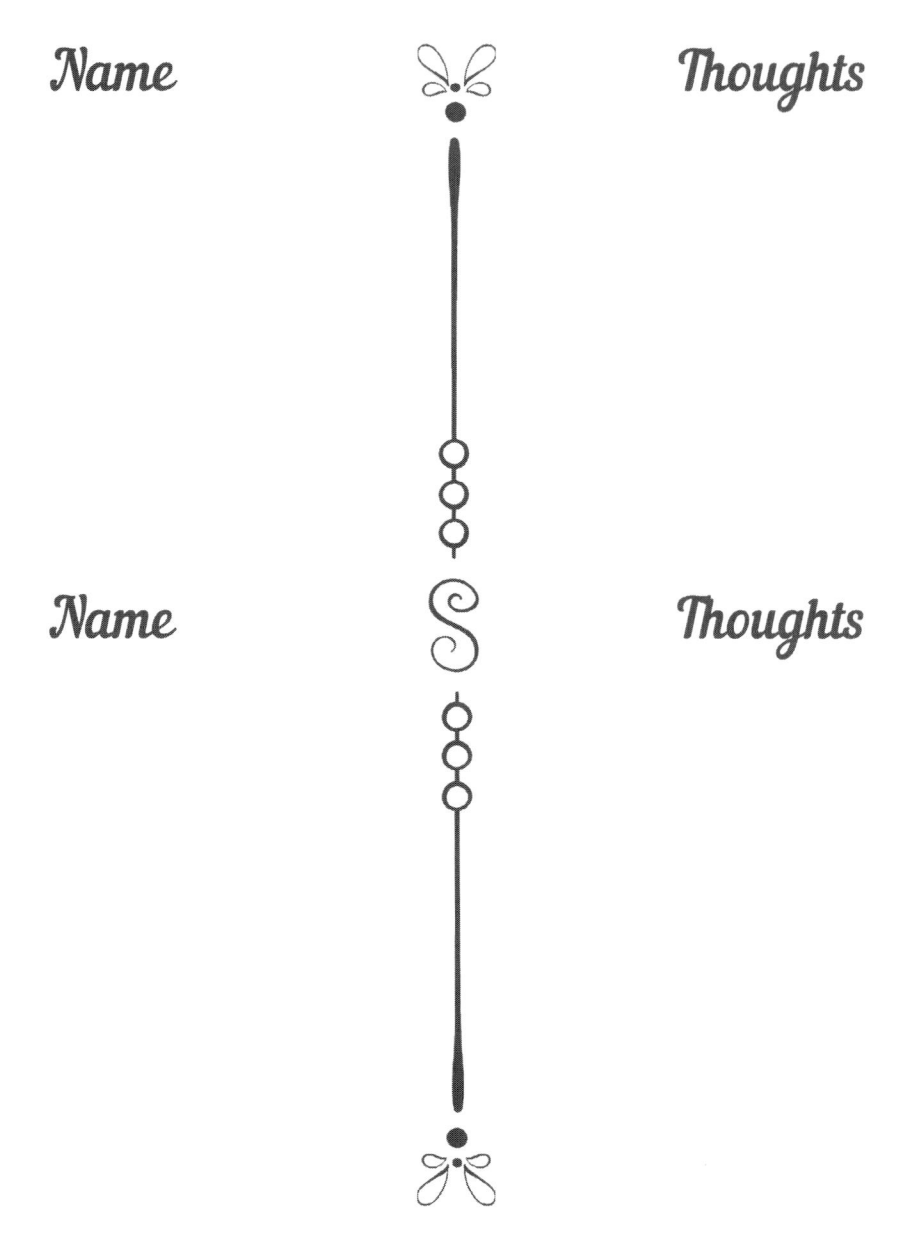

Name   Thoughts

Name   Thoughts

Guests

Name · Thoughts

Name · Thoughts

Guests

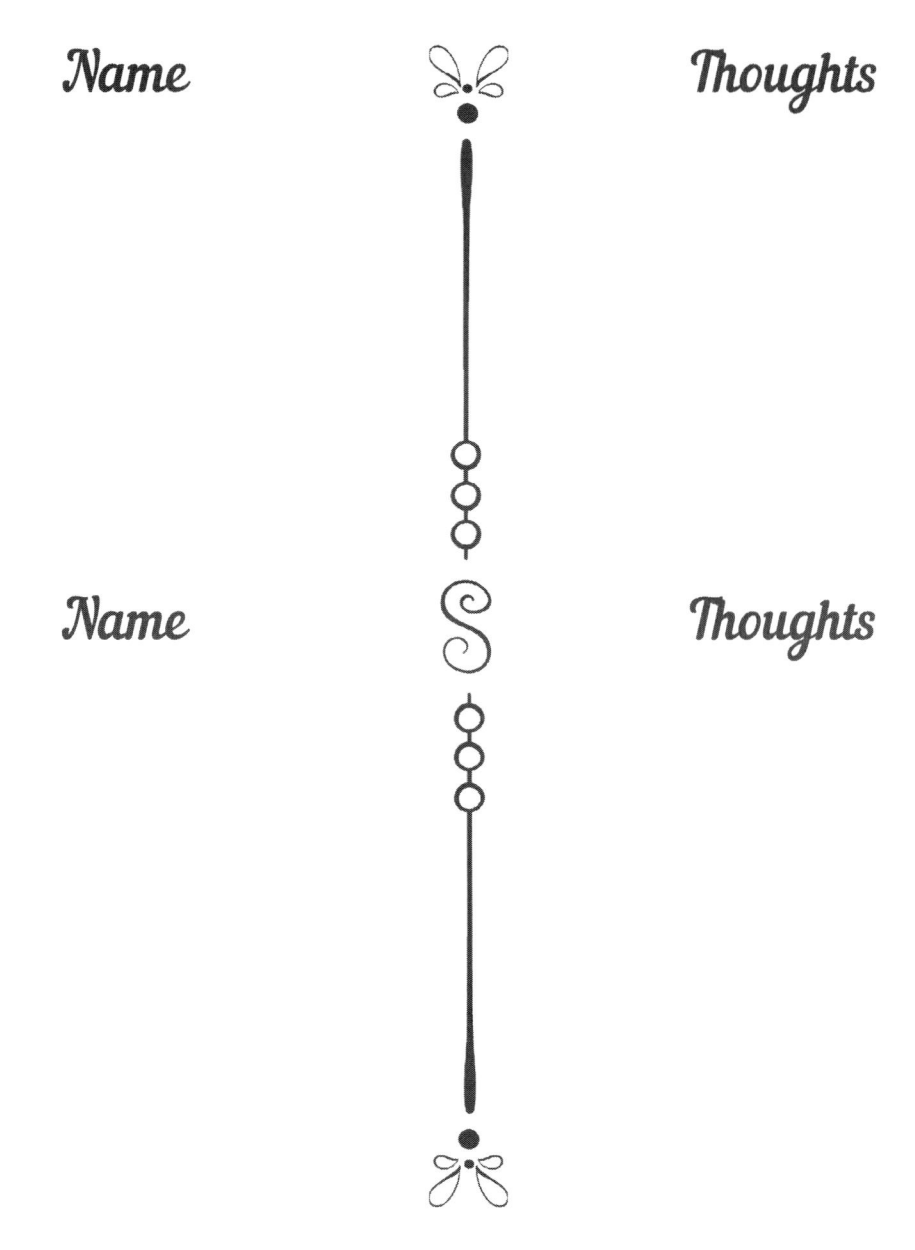

Name Thoughts

Name Thoughts

Guests

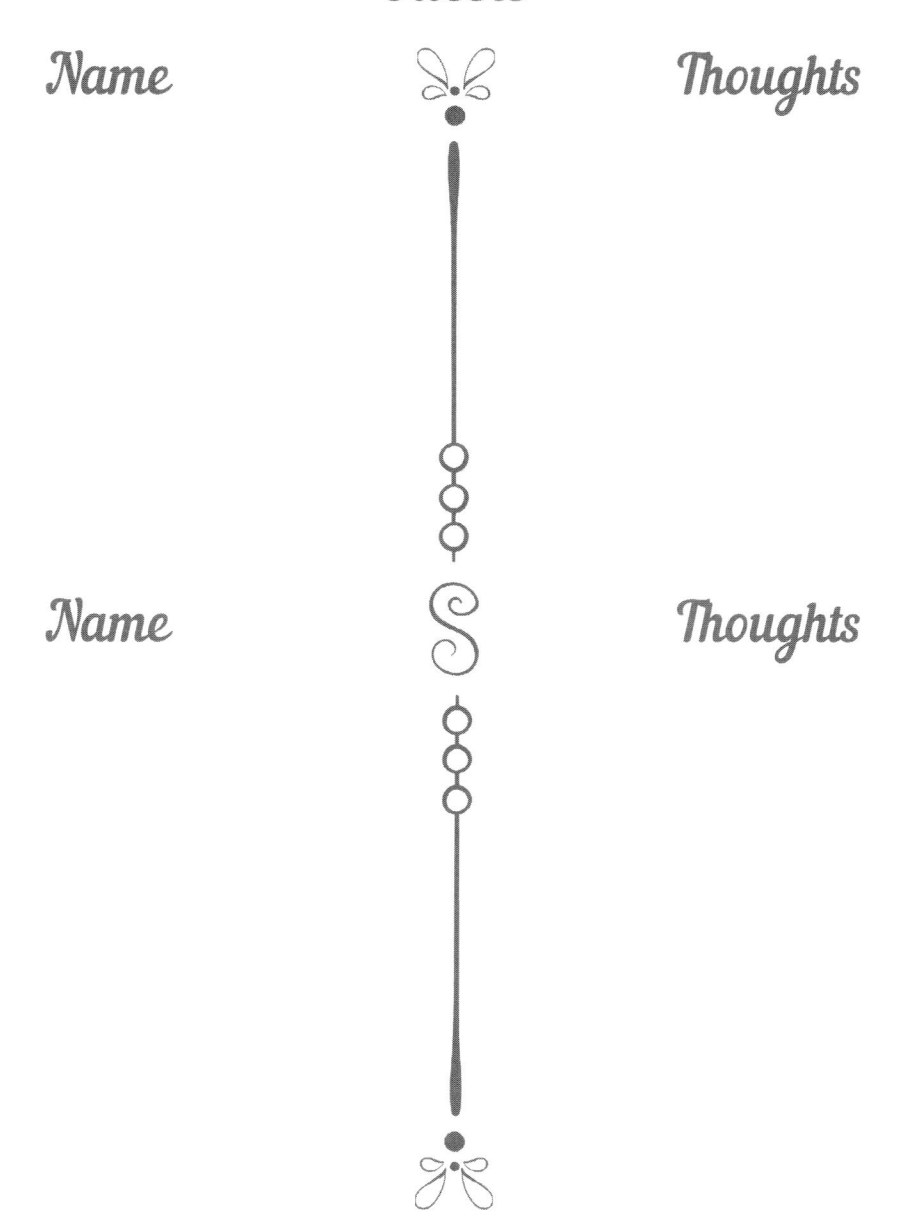

Name — Thoughts

Name — Thoughts

Guests

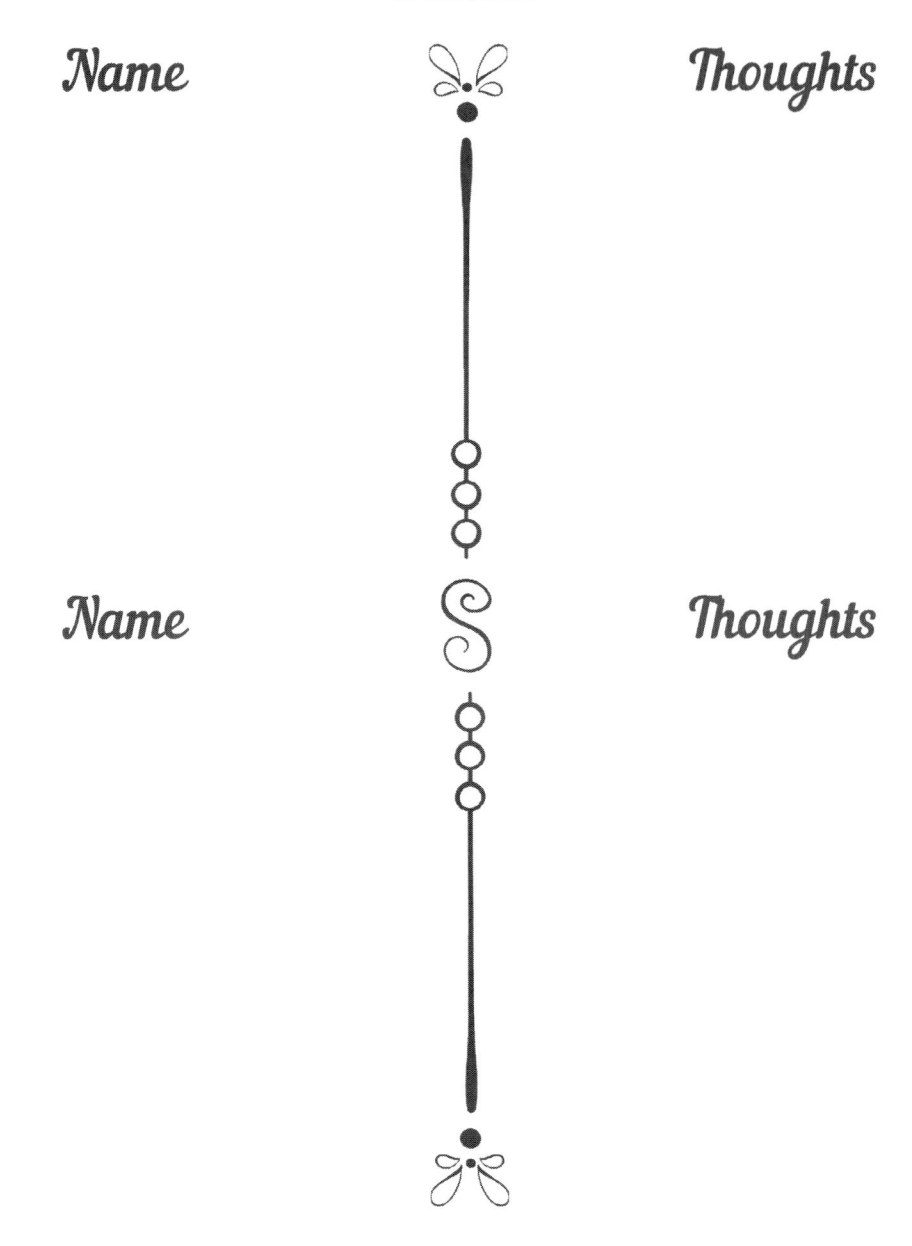

Name   *Thoughts*

Name   *Thoughts*

Guests

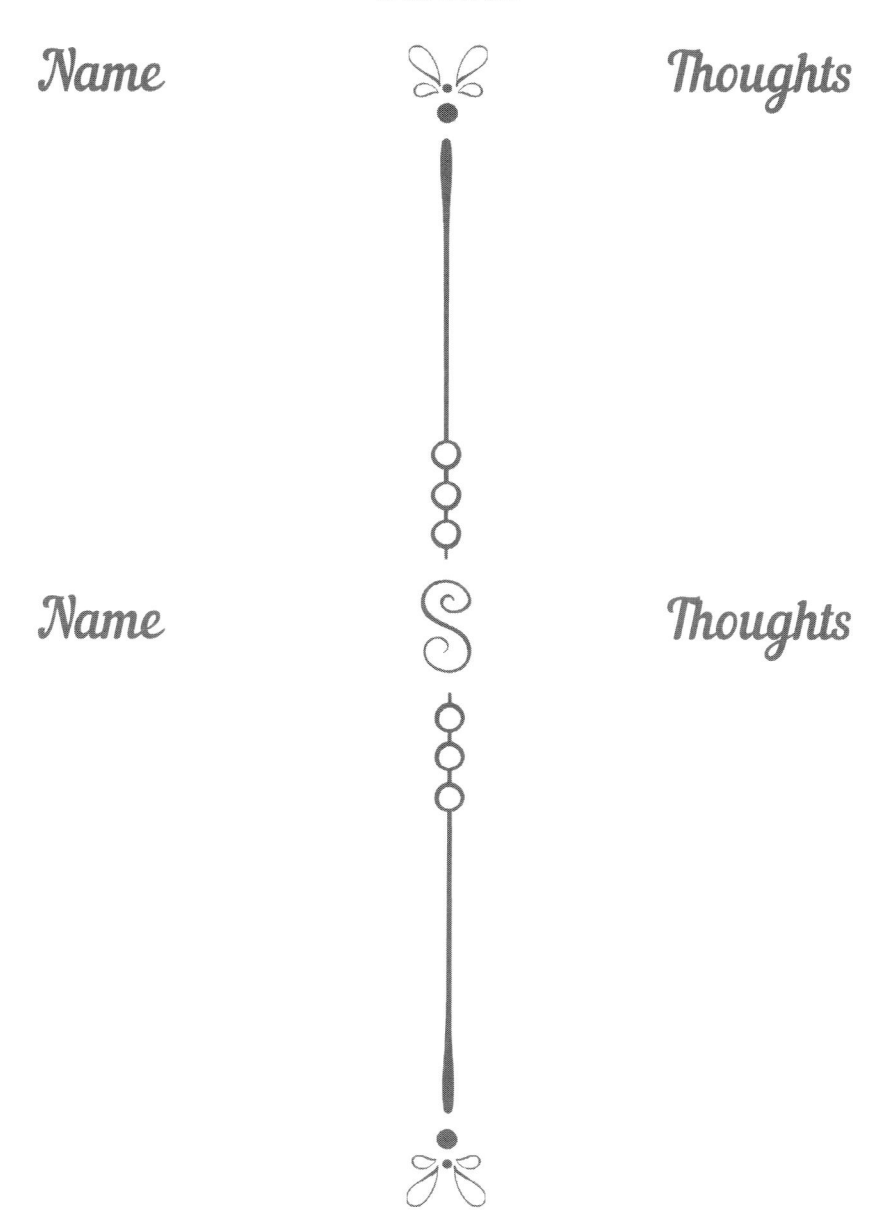

Name　　　　　　　　　　**Thoughts**

Name　　　　　　　　　　**Thoughts**

Guests

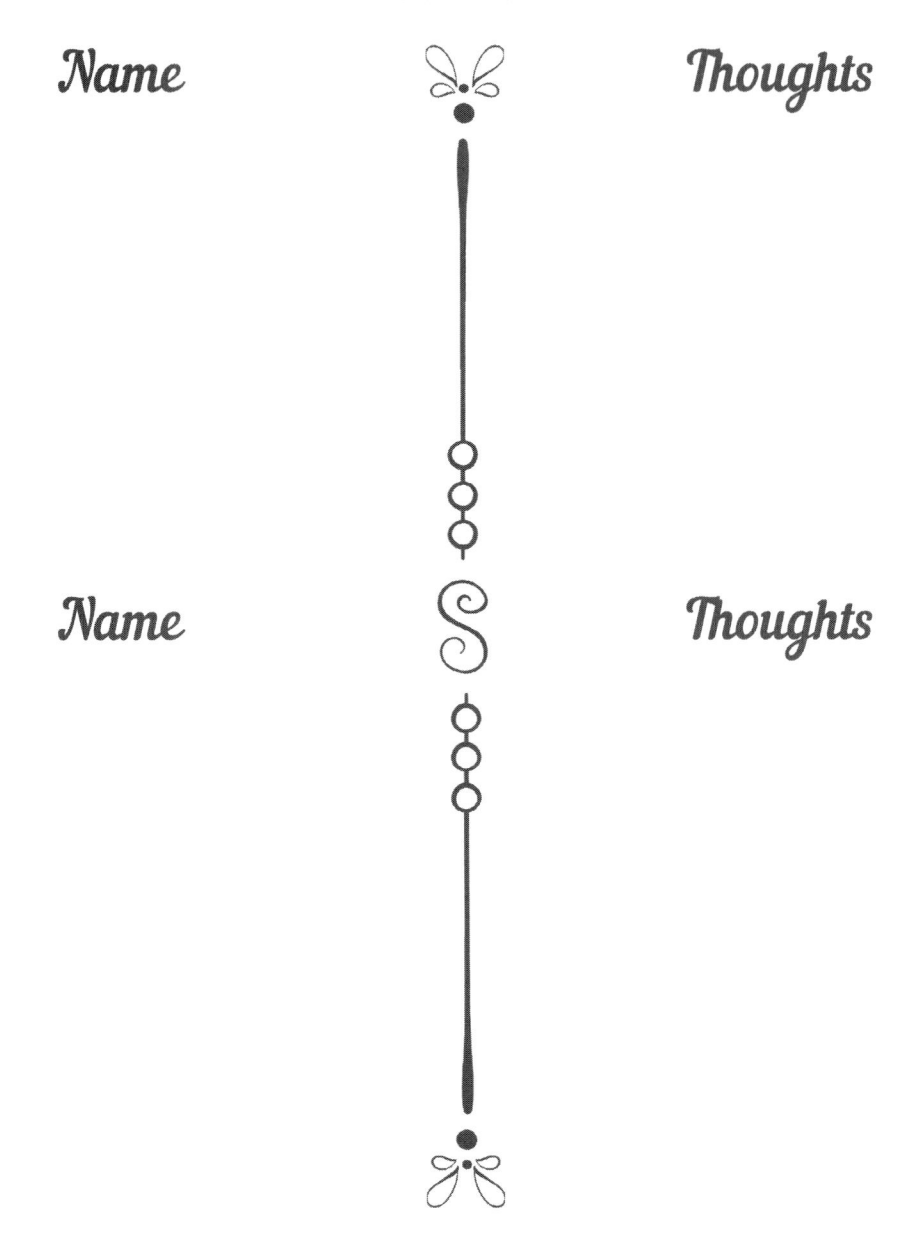

Name Thoughts

Name Thoughts

Guests

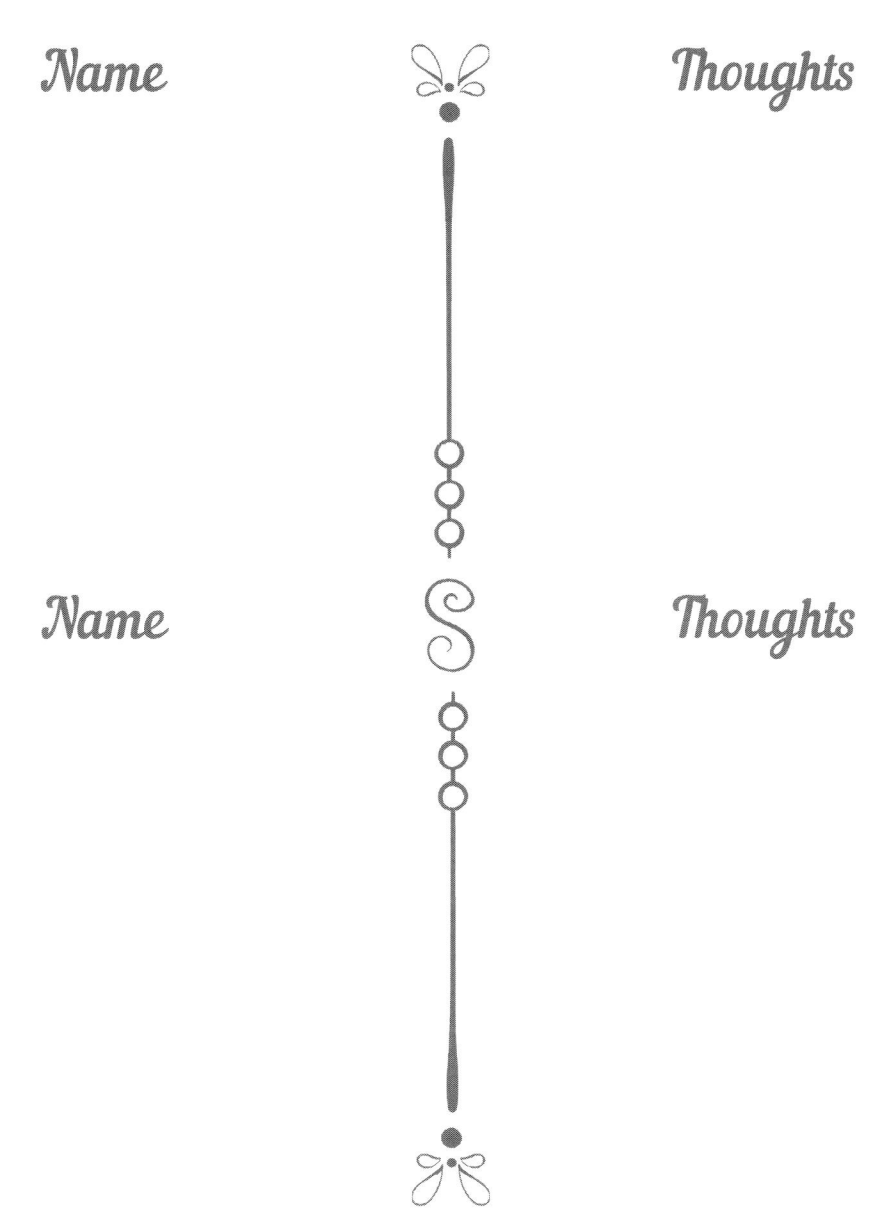

Name | Thoughts

Name | Thoughts

Guests

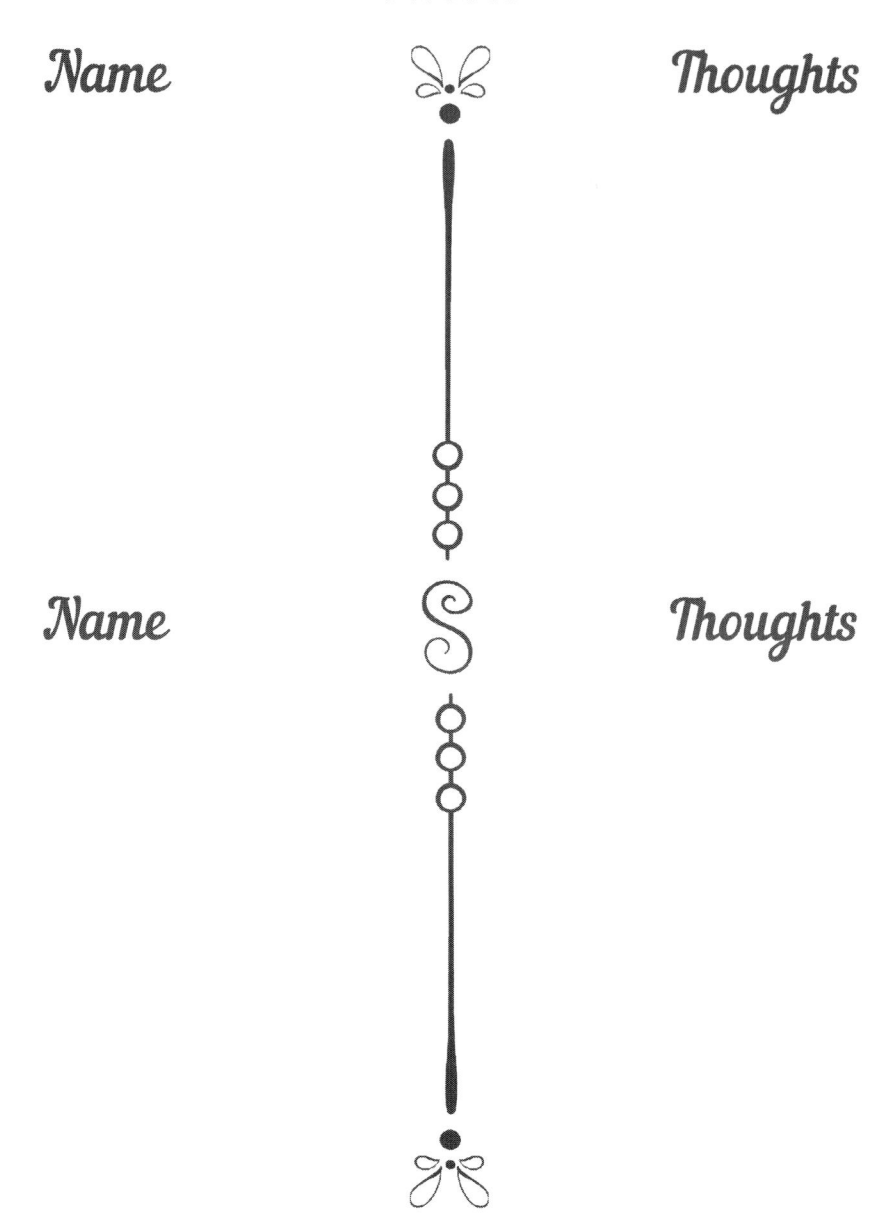

Name · Thoughts

Name · Thoughts

Guests

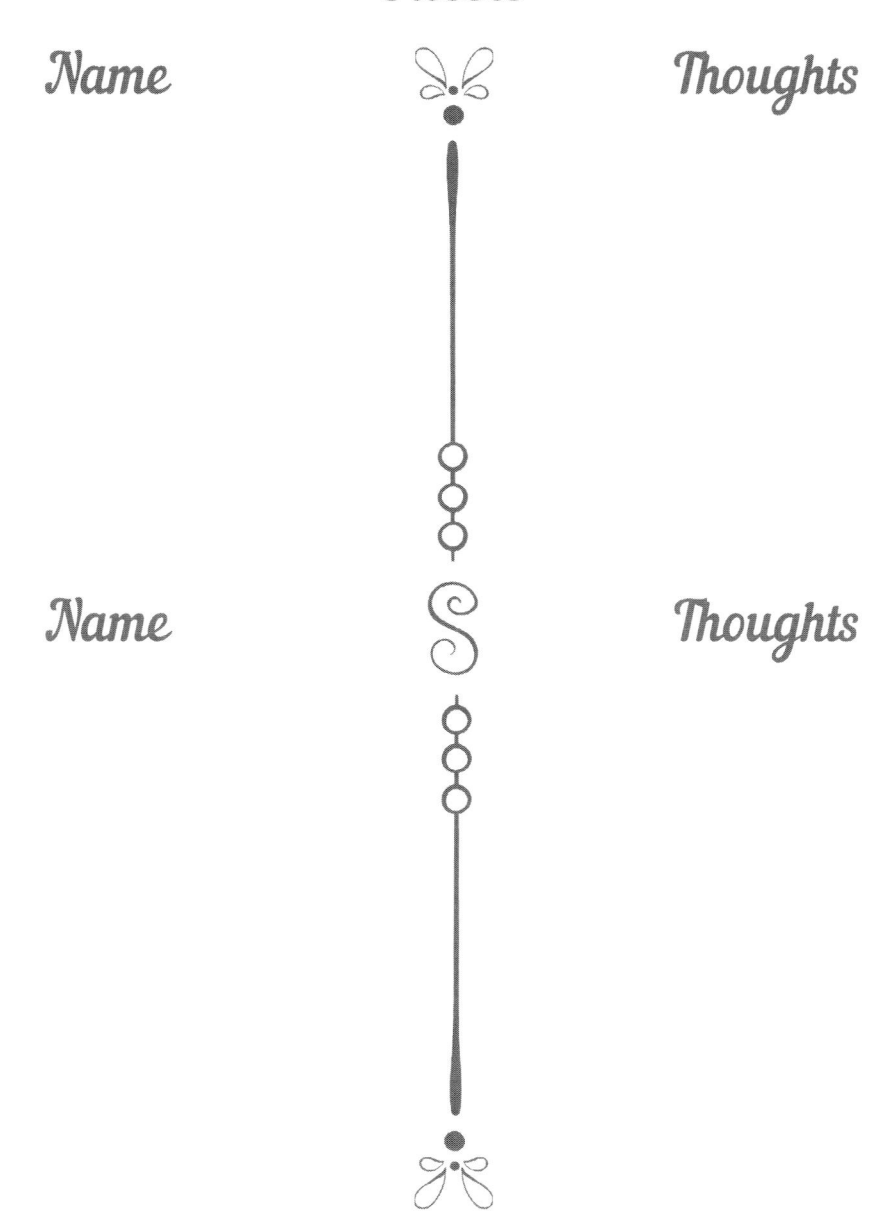

Name · Thoughts

Name · Thoughts

Guests

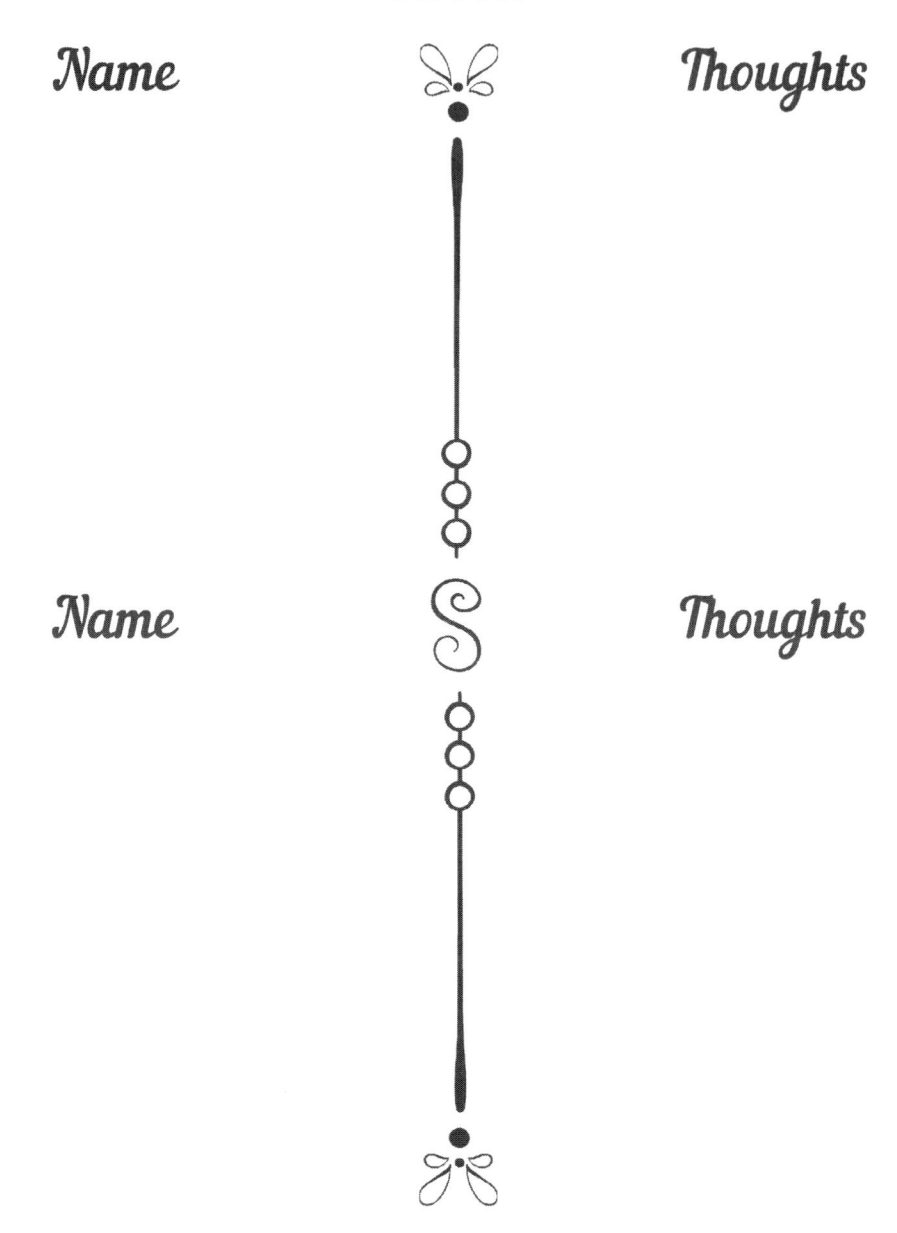

Name Thoughts

Name Thoughts

Guests

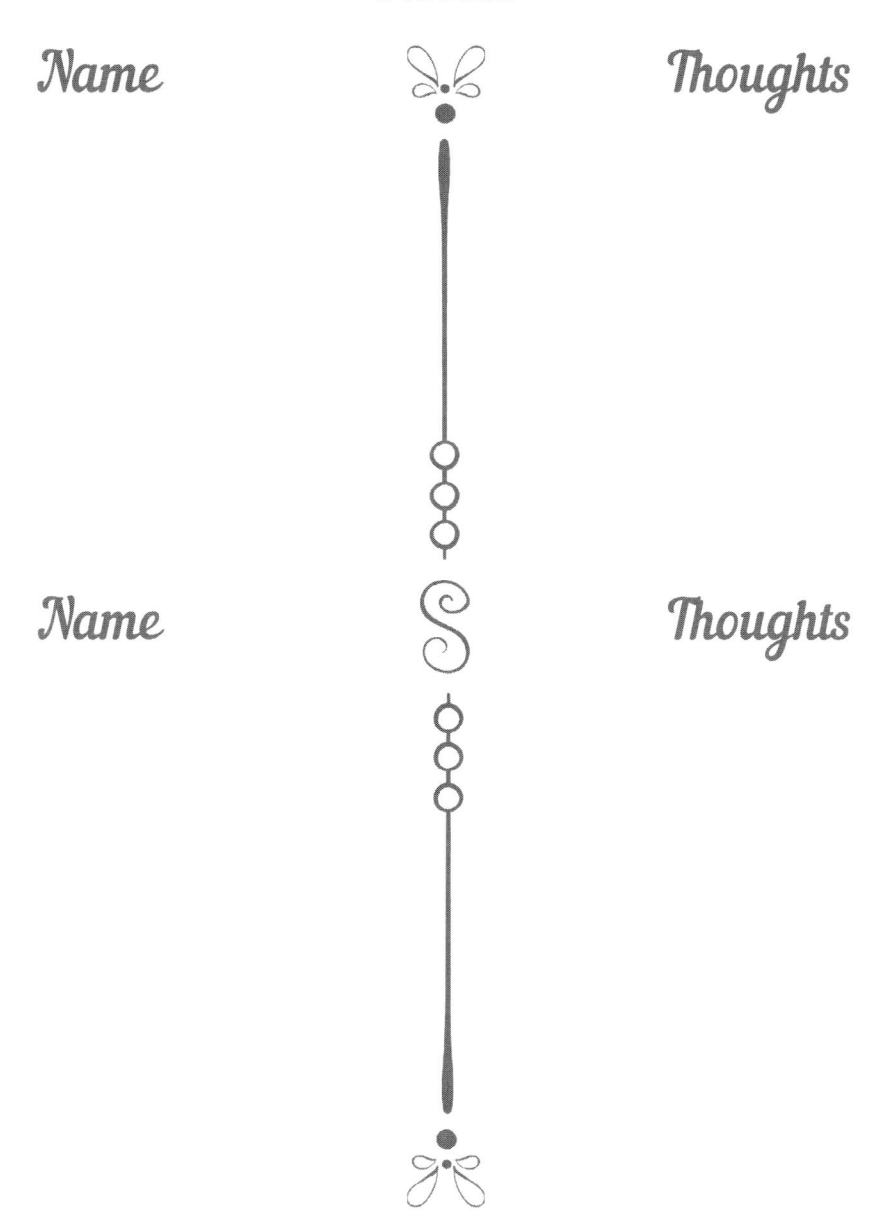

Name   Thoughts

Name   Thoughts

Guests

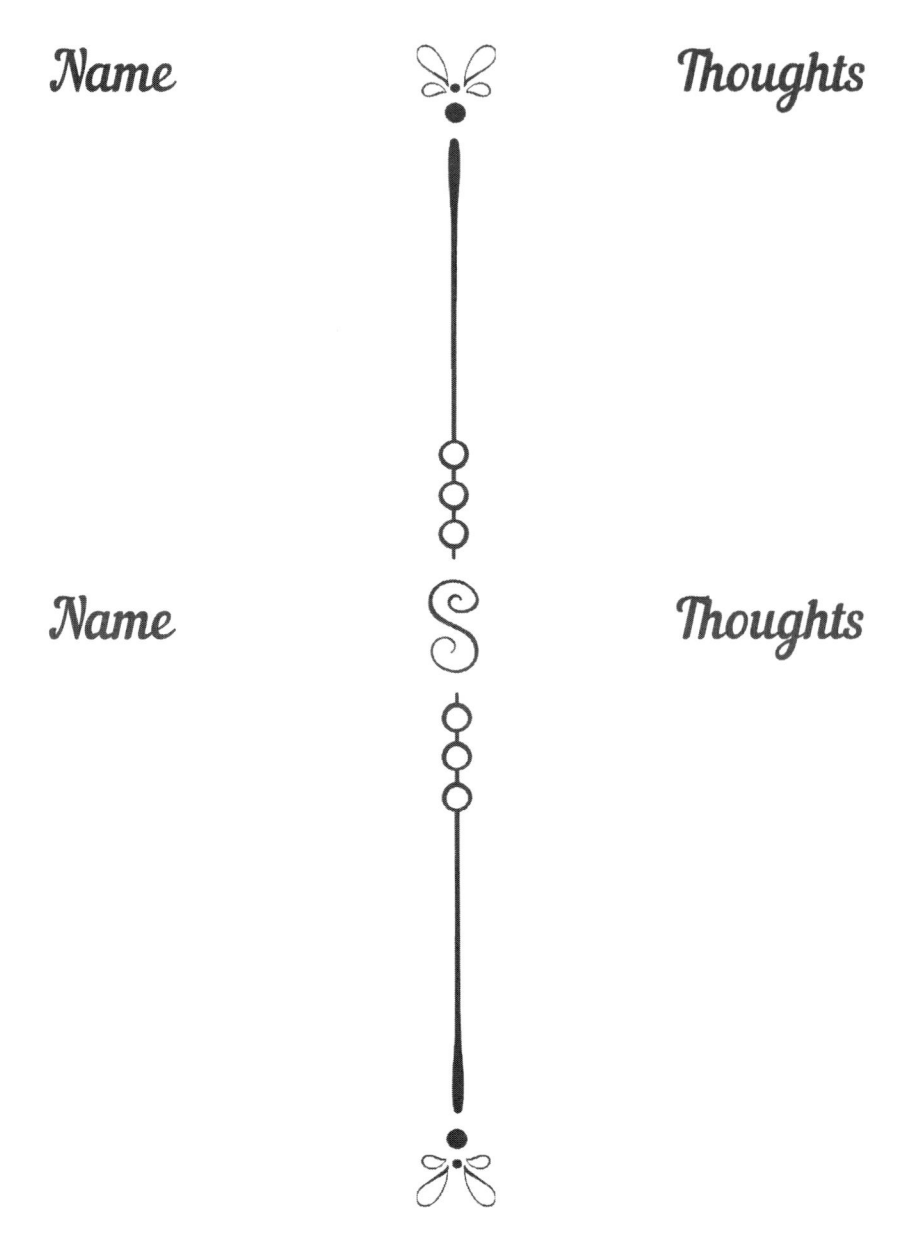

Name   *Thoughts*

Name   *Thoughts*

Guests

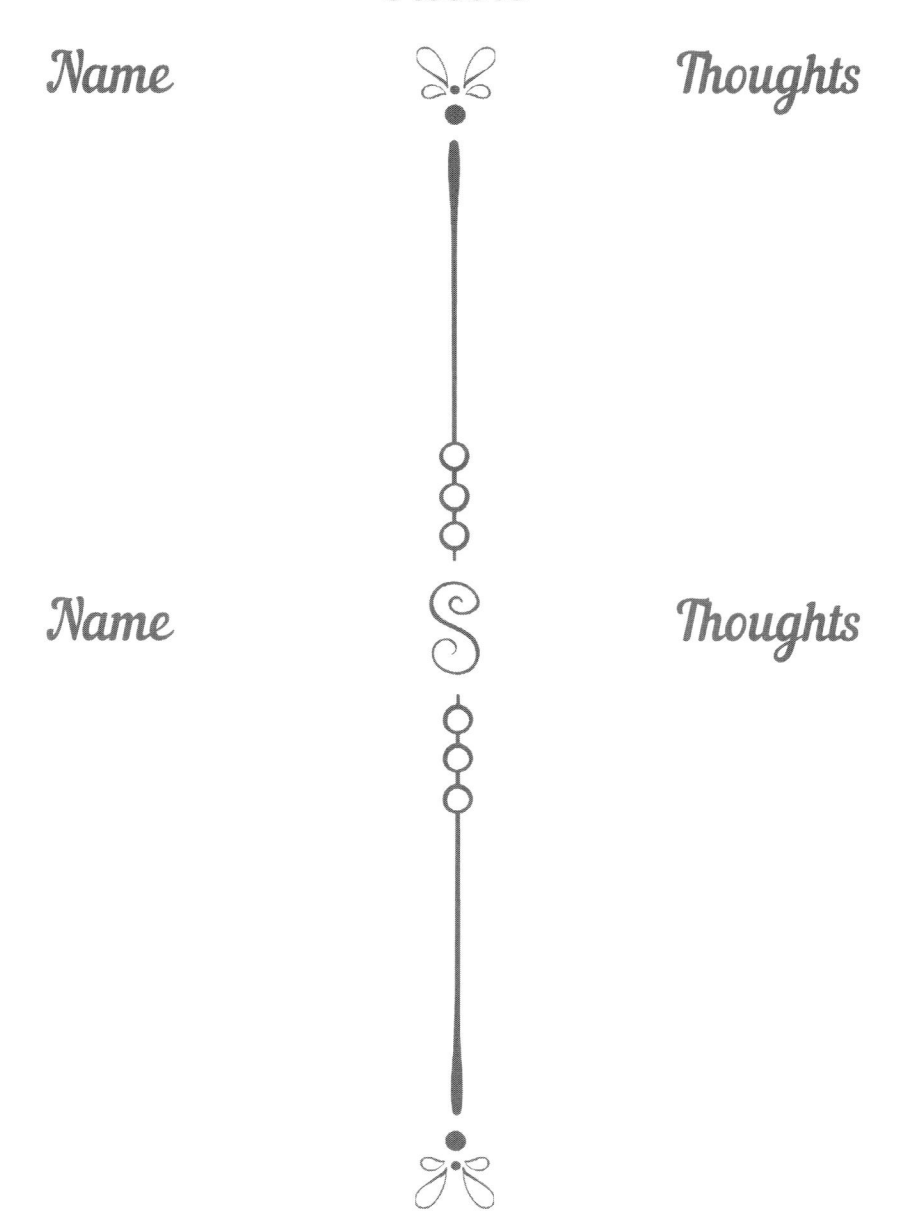

Name · Thoughts

Name · Thoughts

Guests

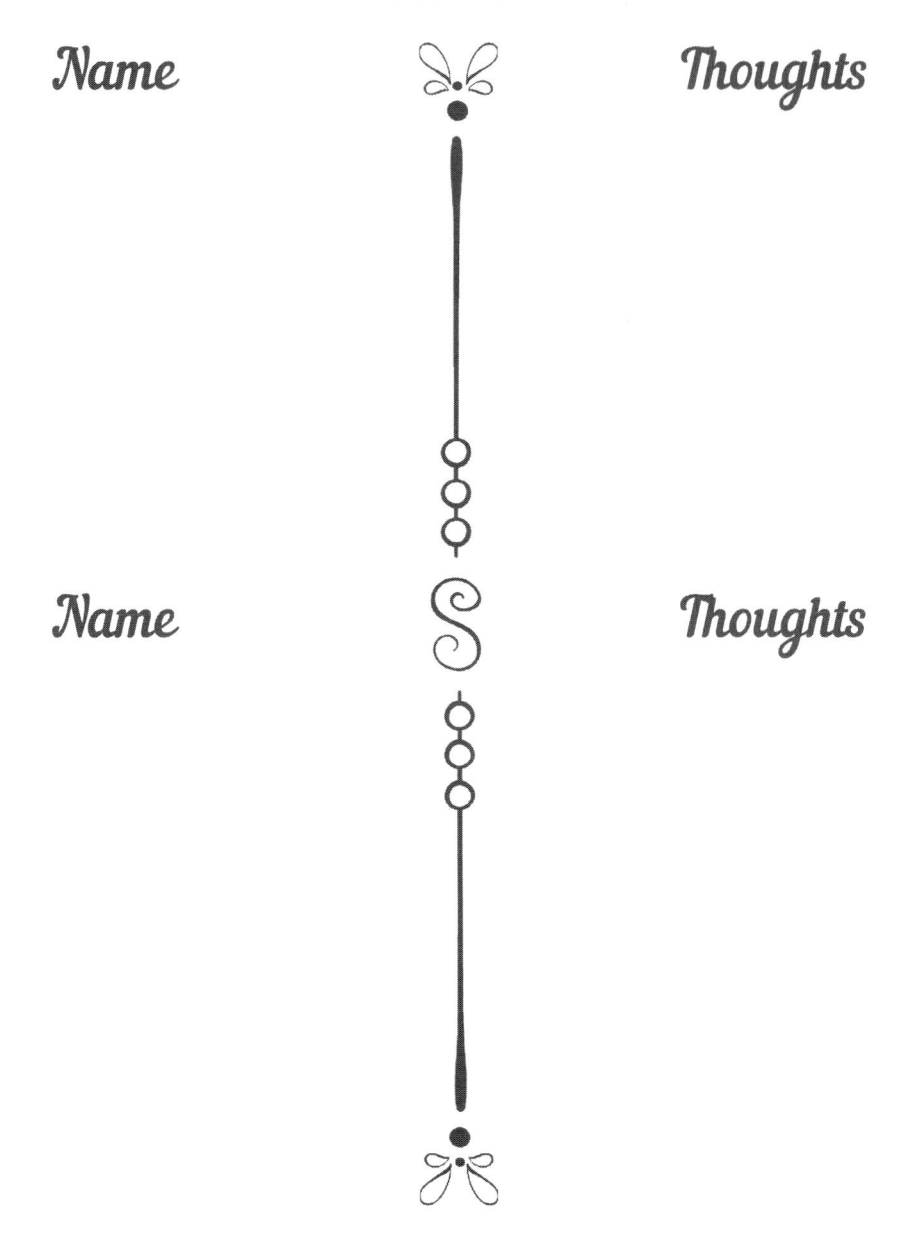

Name Thoughts

Name Thoughts

Guests

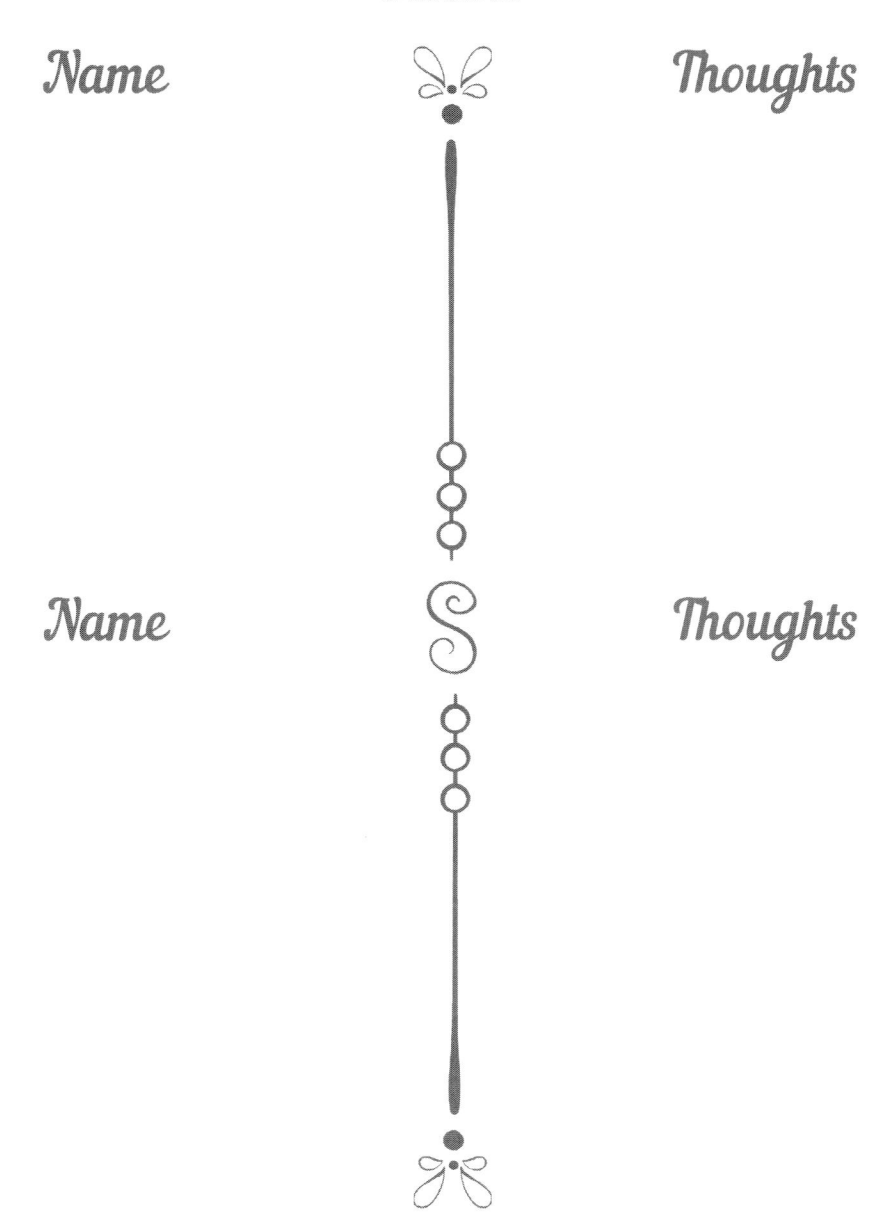

Name · Thoughts

Name · Thoughts

Guests

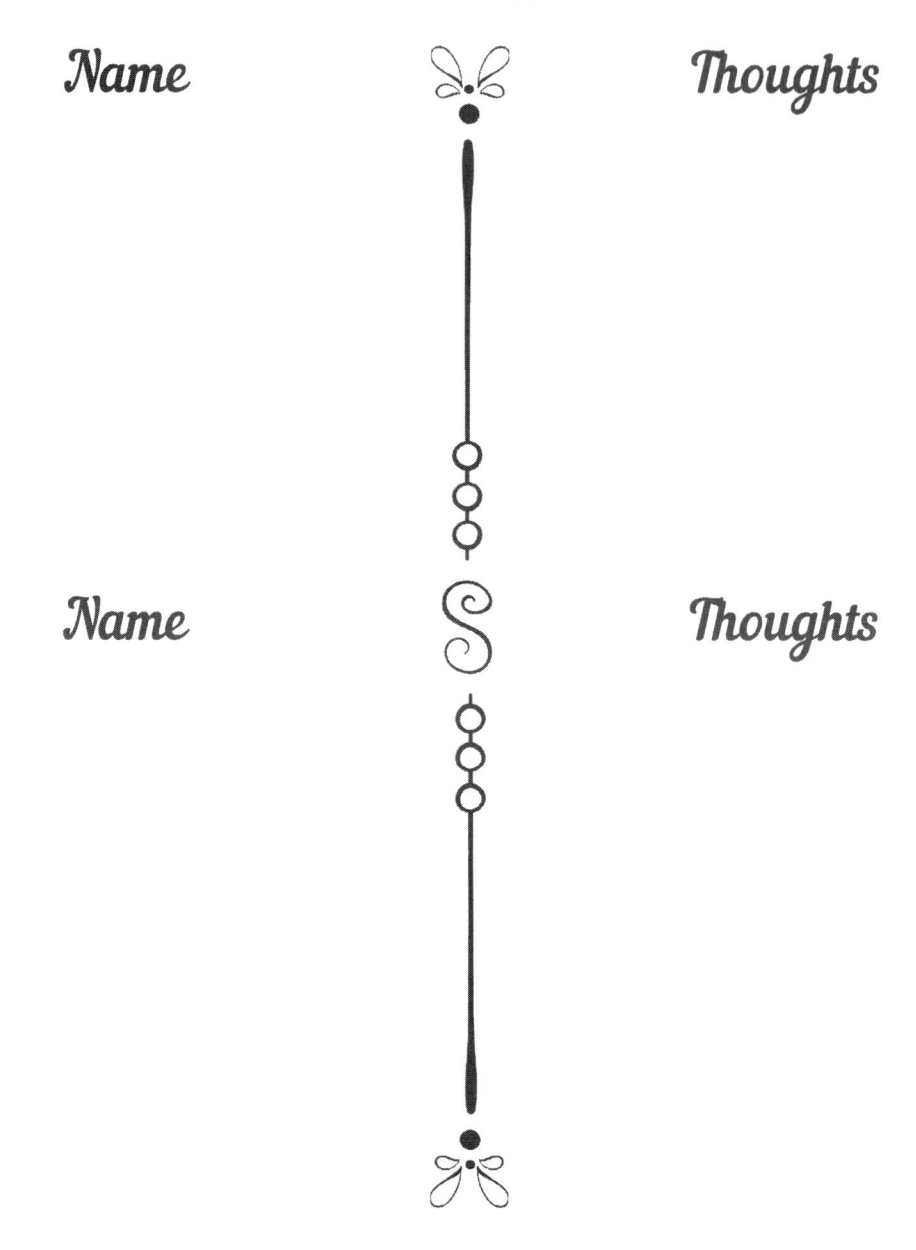

Name   *Thoughts*

Name   *Thoughts*

Guests

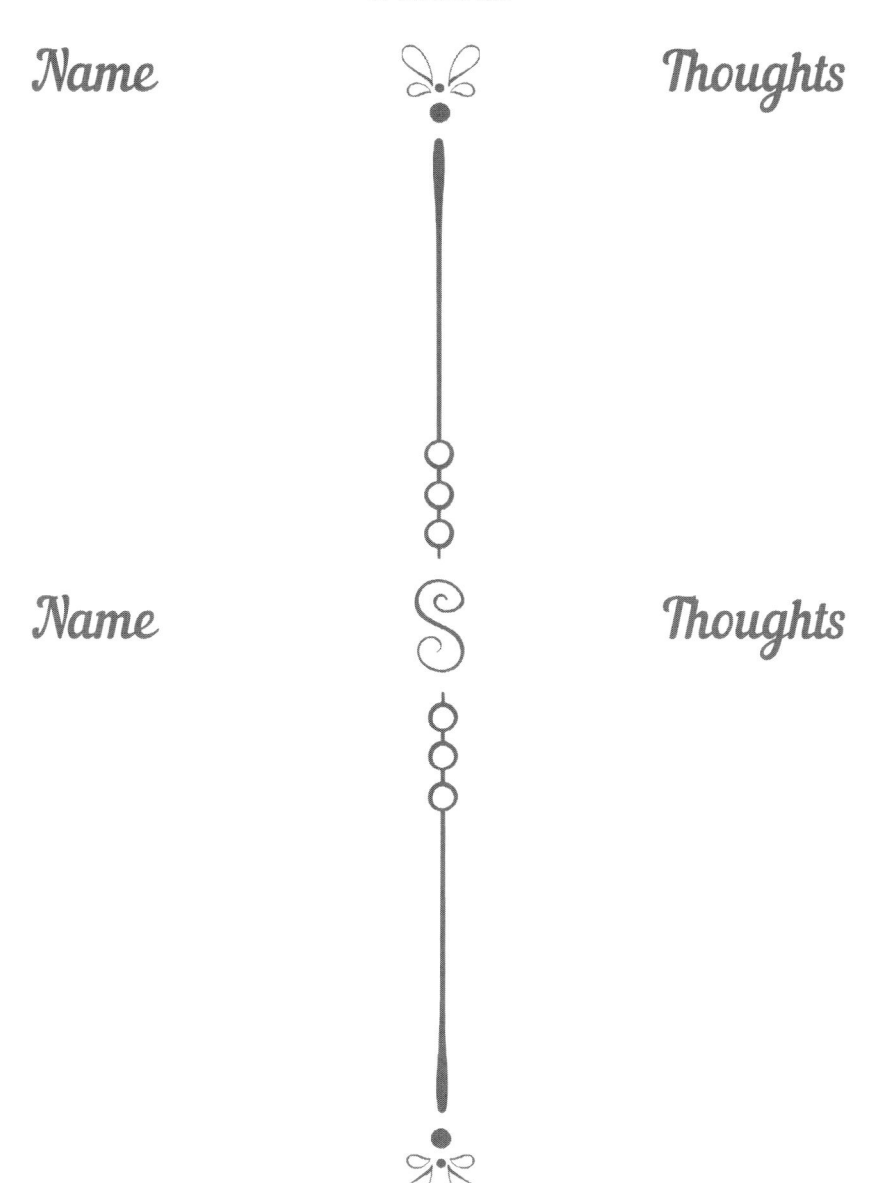

Name   Thoughts

Name   Thoughts

Guests

Name   Thoughts

Name   Thoughts

Guests

Name　　　　　　　　　　Thoughts

Name　　　　　　　　　　Thoughts

Guests

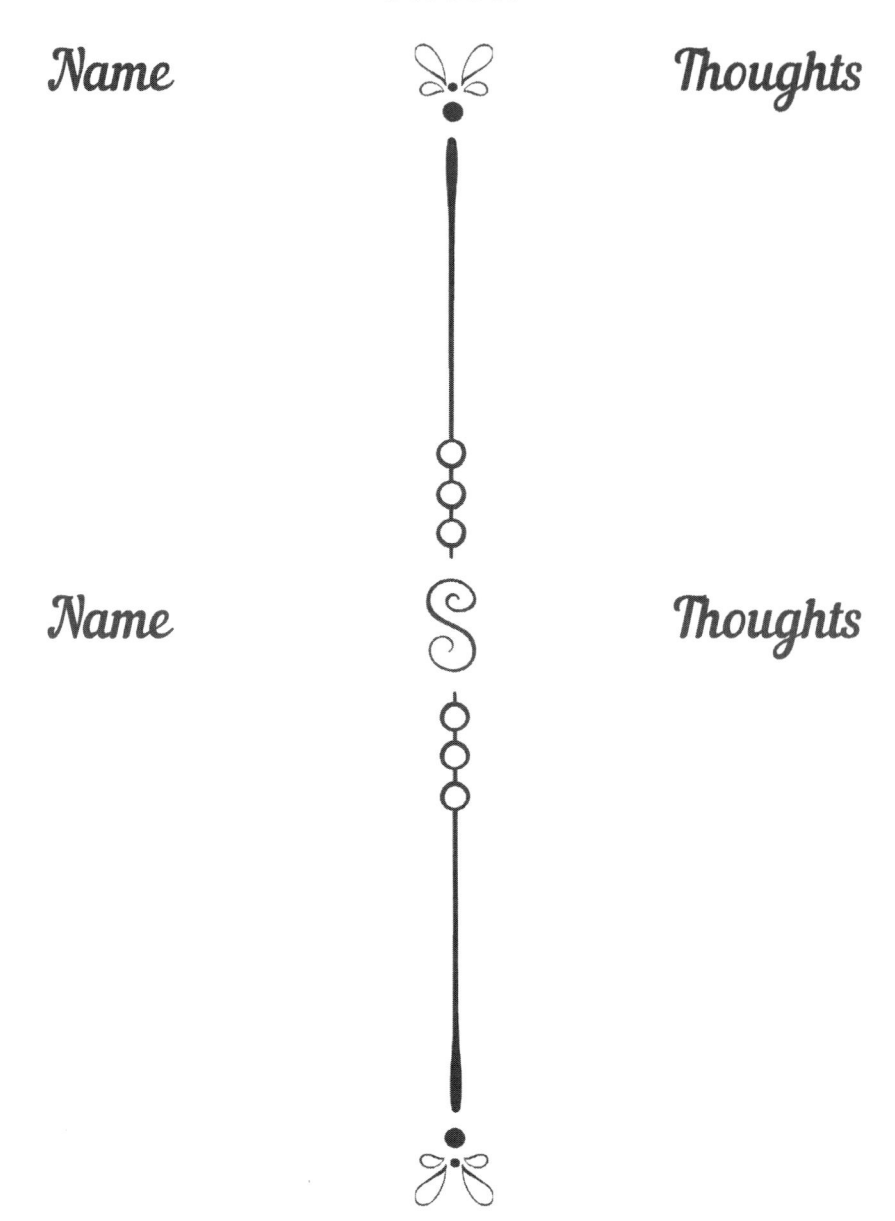

Name   *Thoughts*

Name   *Thoughts*

Guests

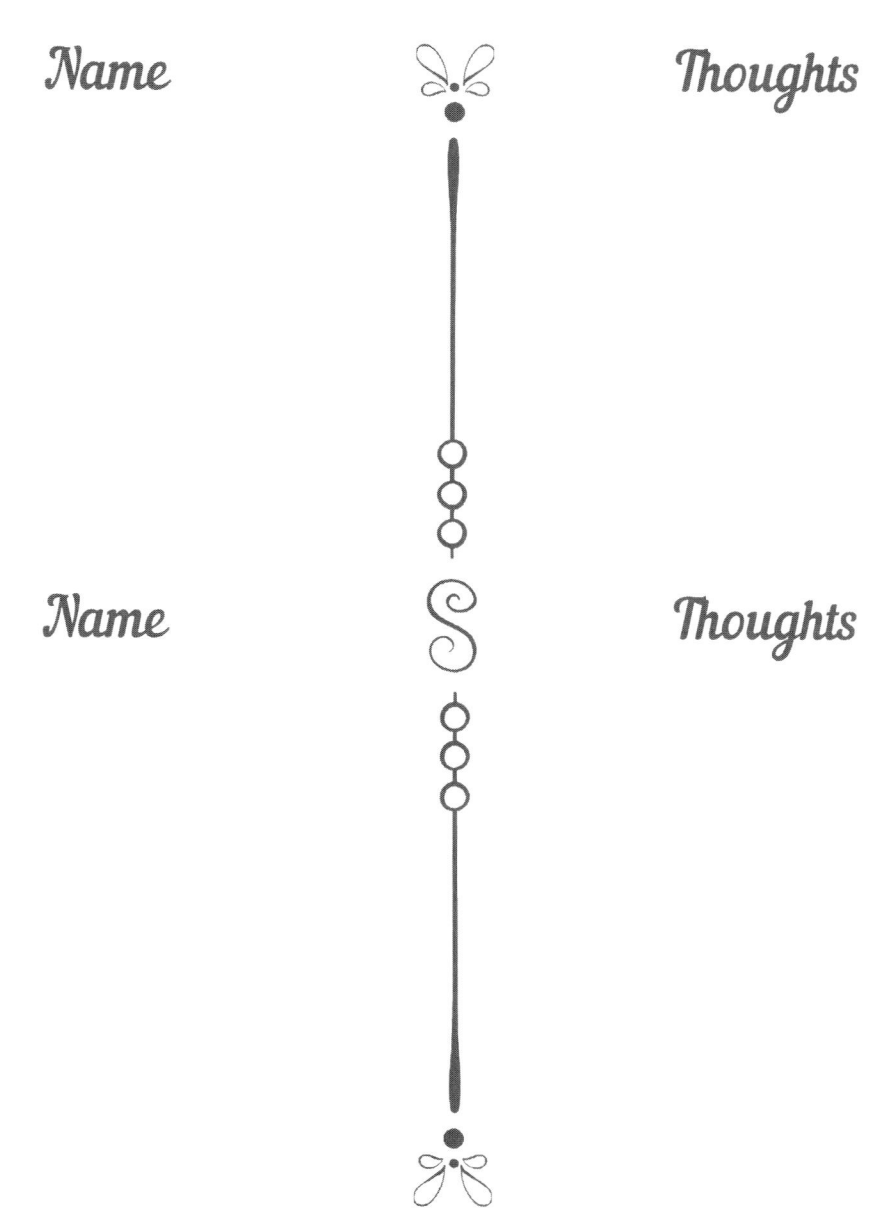

Name　　　　　　　　　　　Thoughts

Name　　　　　　　　　　　Thoughts

Guests

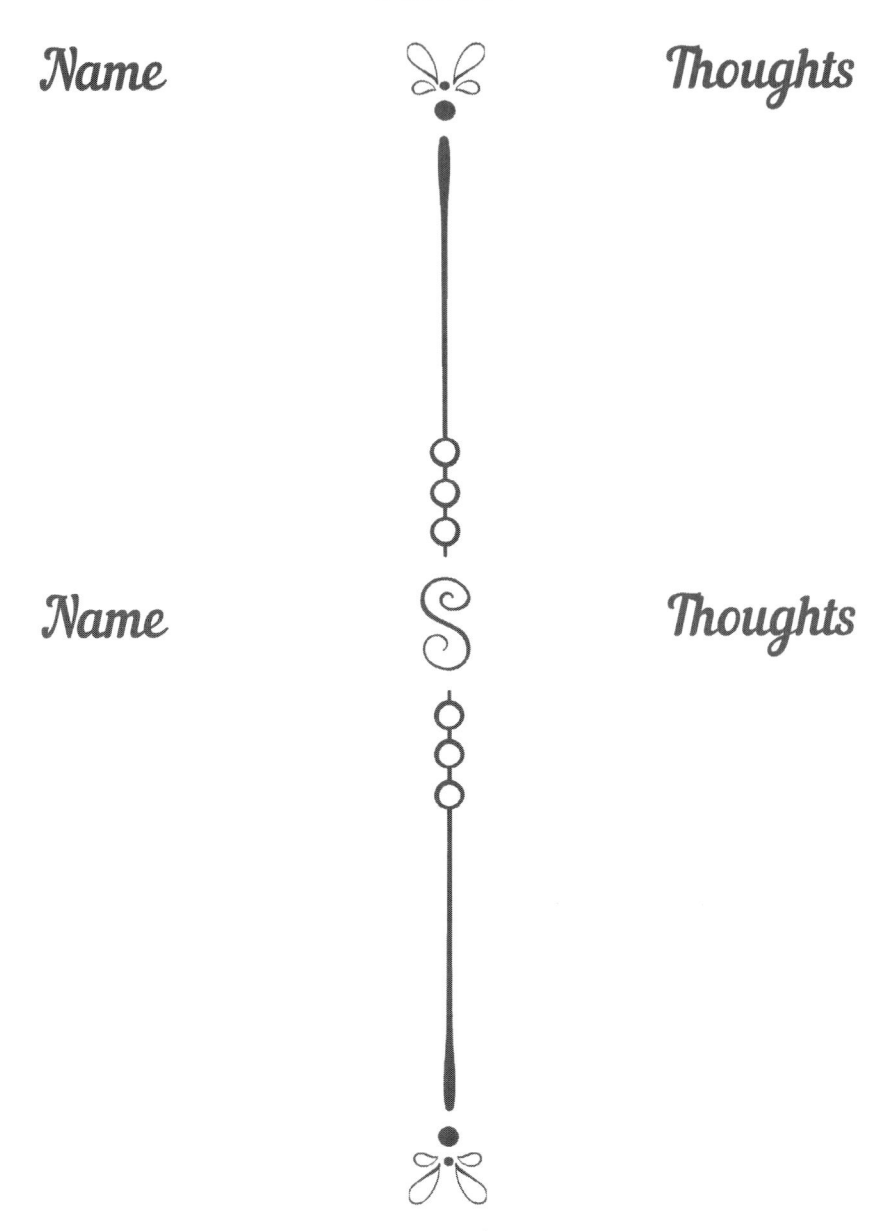

Name — Thoughts

Name — Thoughts

Guests

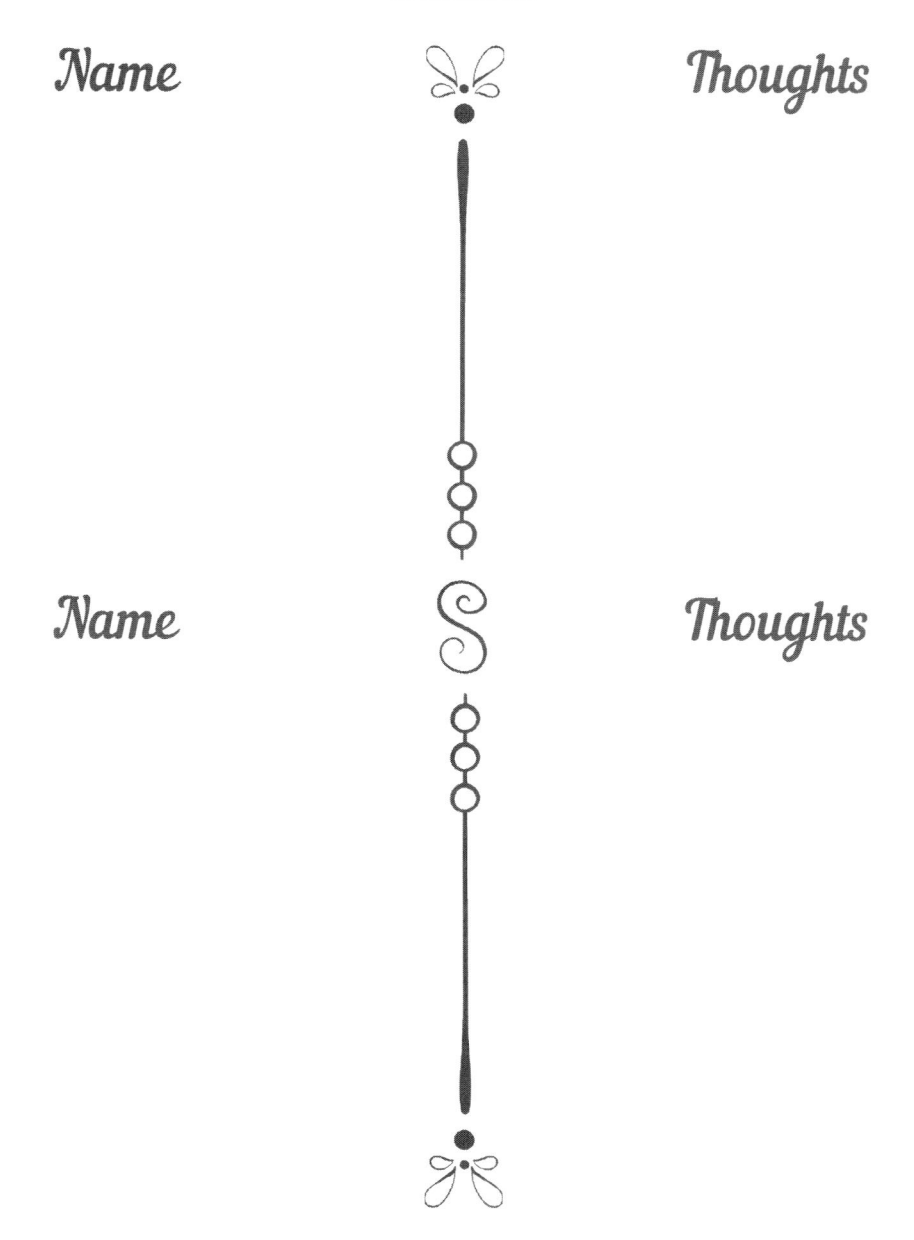

Name   Thoughts

Name   Thoughts

Guests

Name　　　　　Thoughts

Name　　　S　　　Thoughts

Guests

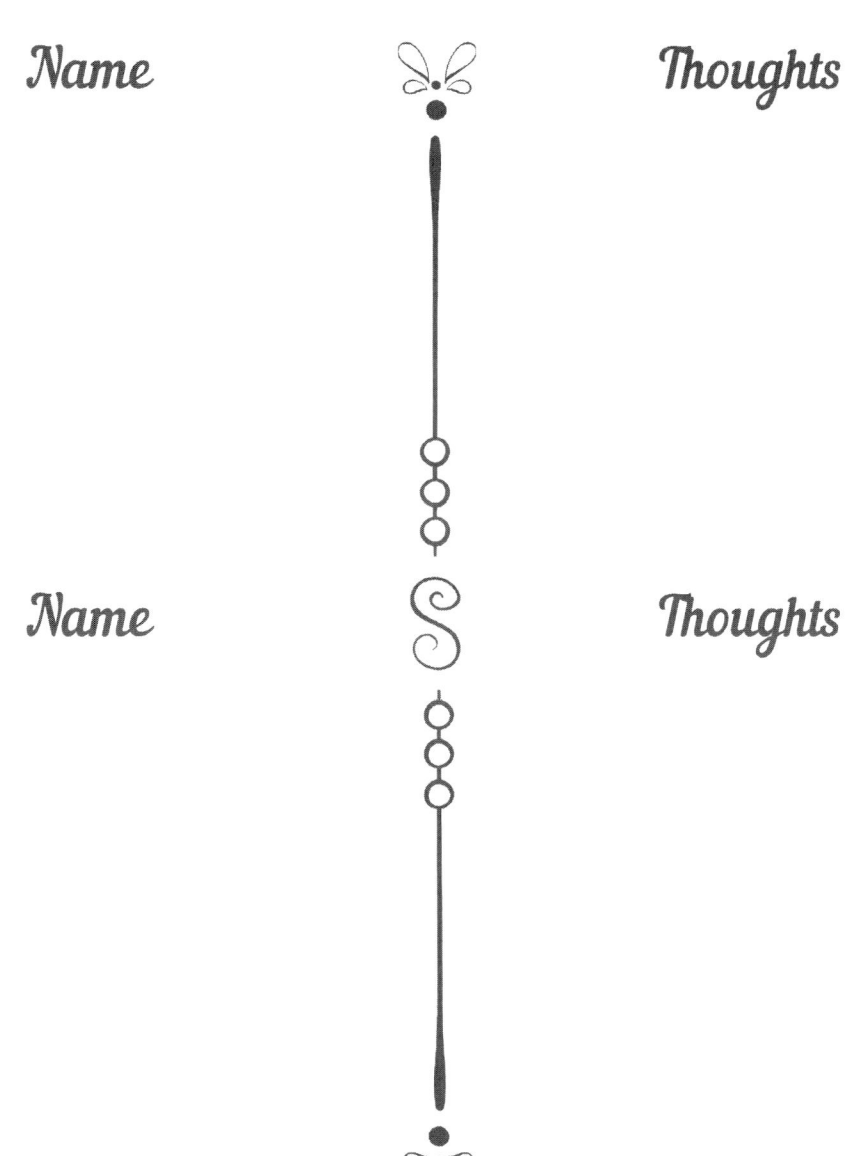

Name   Thoughts

Name   Thoughts

Guests

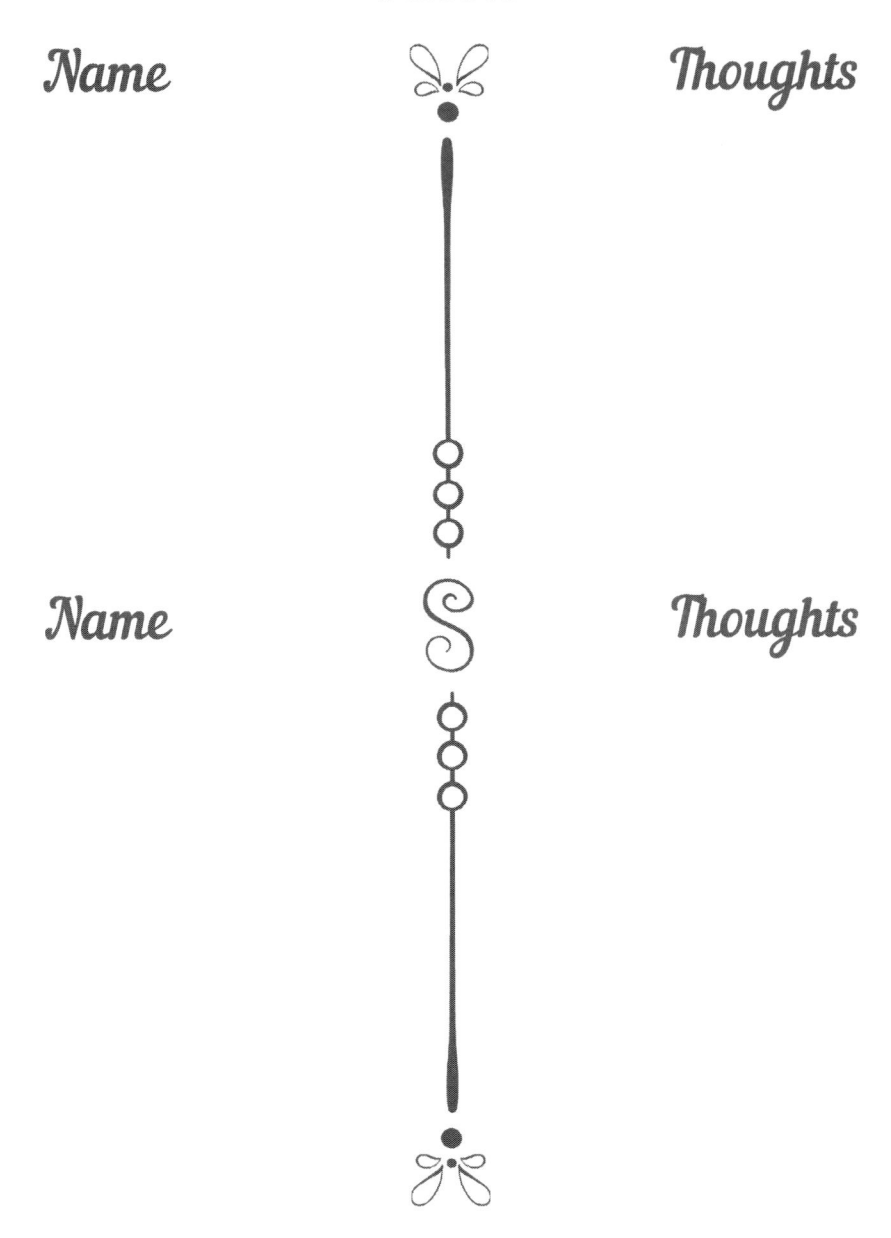

Name — Thoughts

Name — Thoughts

Guests

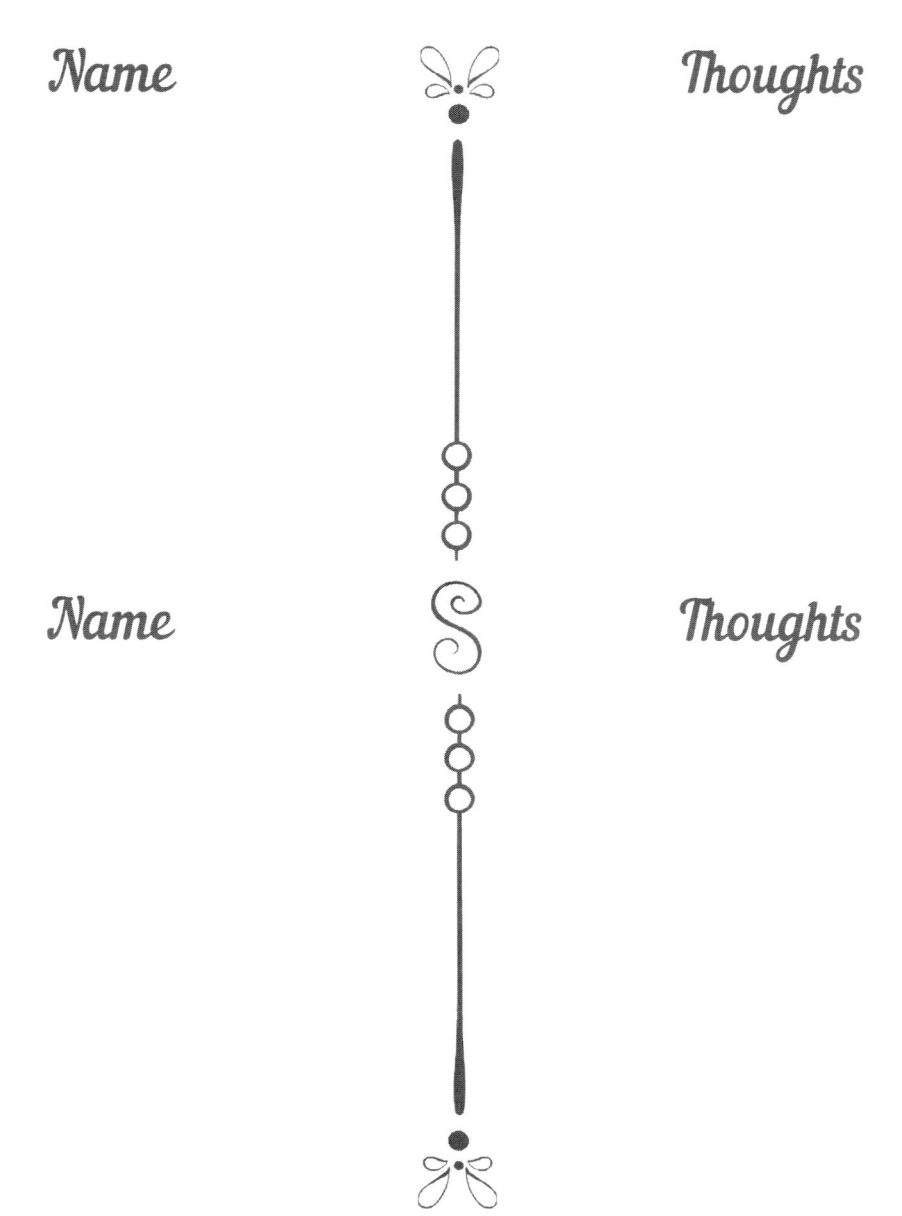

Name   Thoughts

Name   Thoughts

Guests

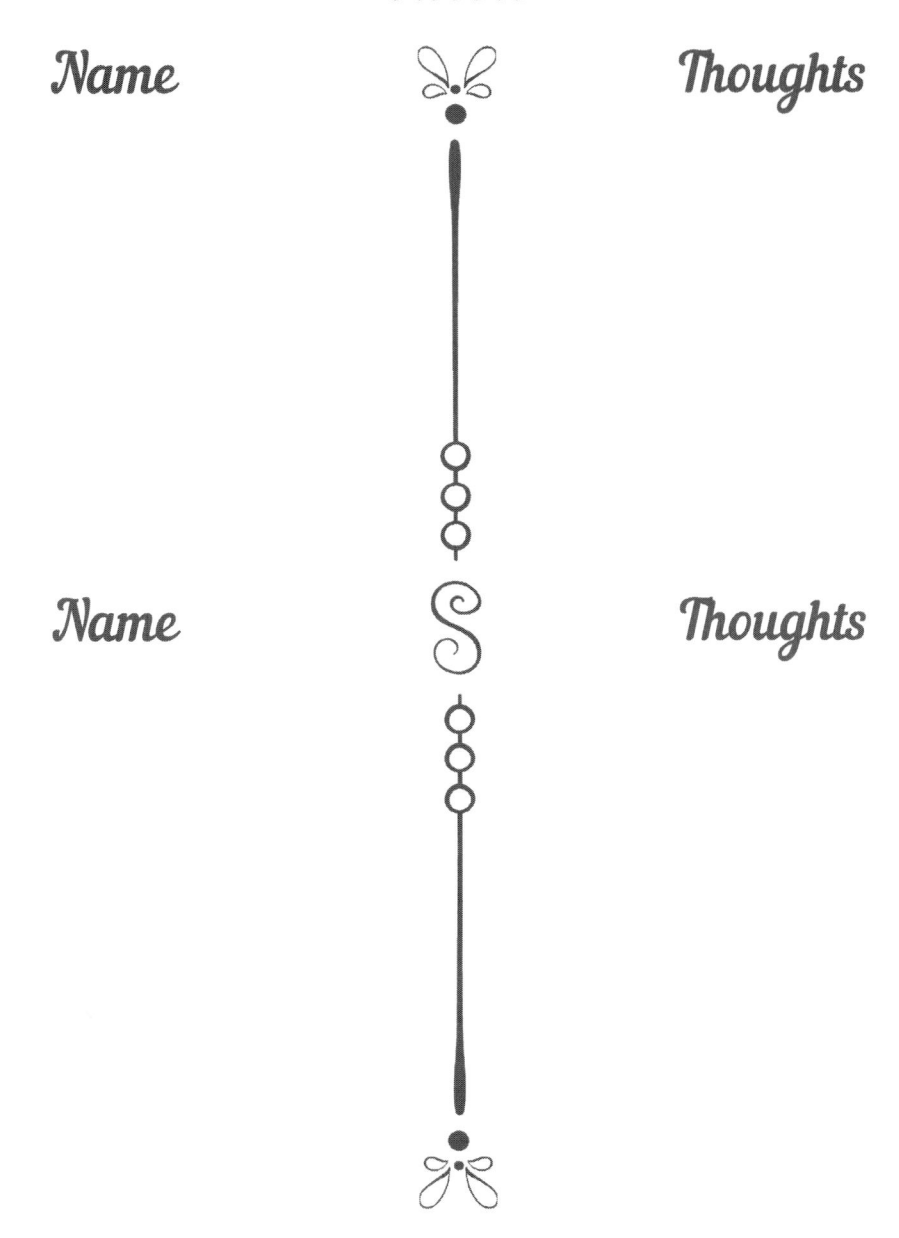

Name · Thoughts

Name · Thoughts

Guests

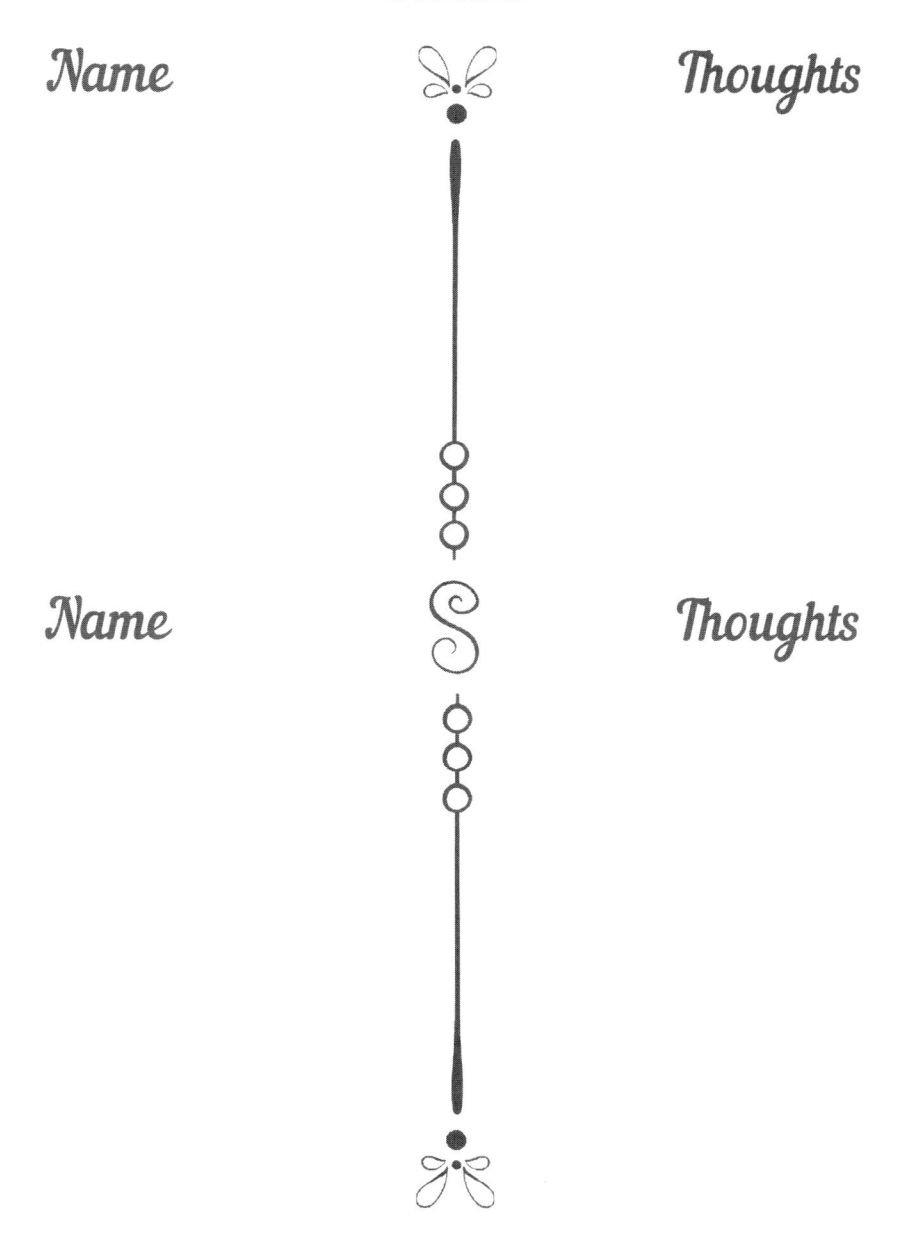

Name Thoughts

Name Thoughts

Guests

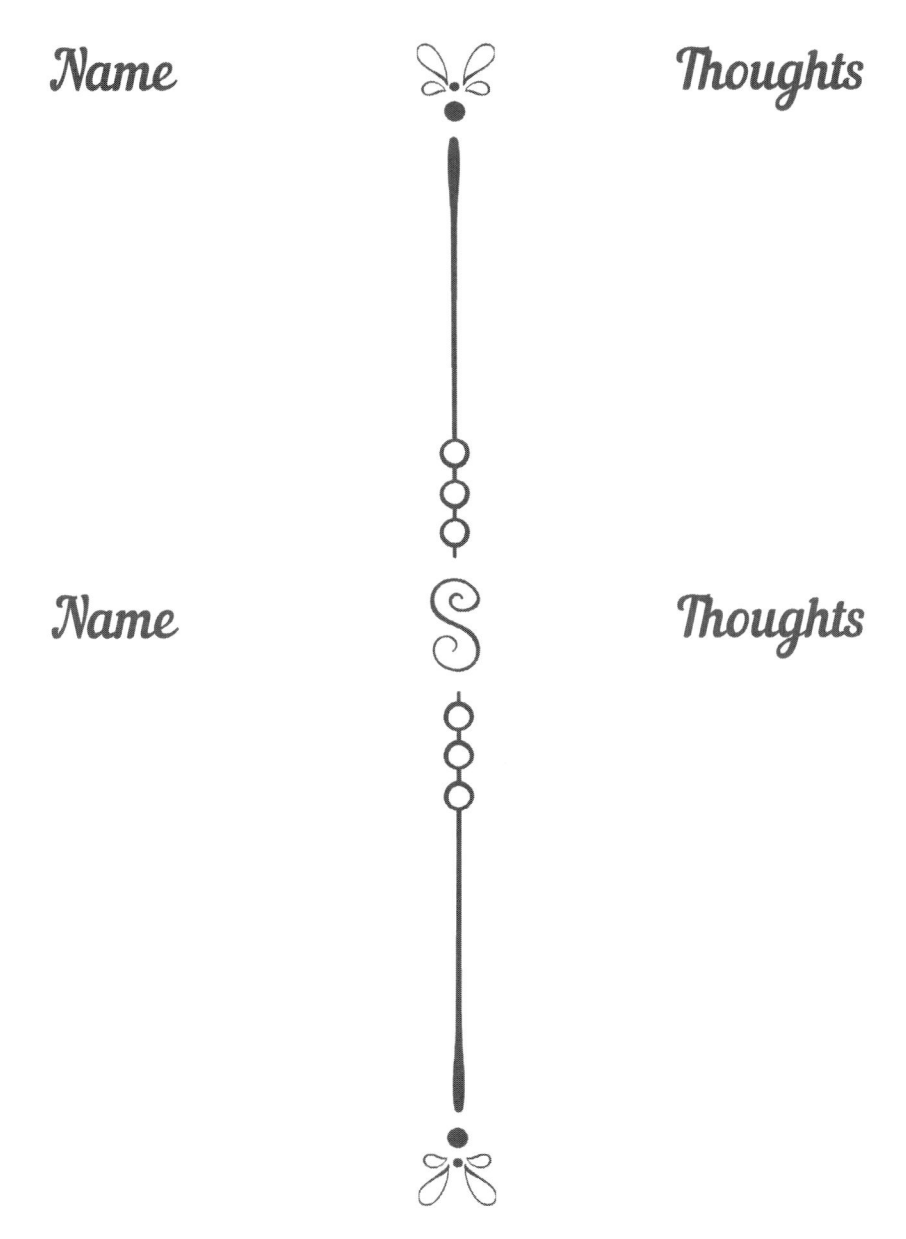

Name						Thoughts

Name						Thoughts

Guests

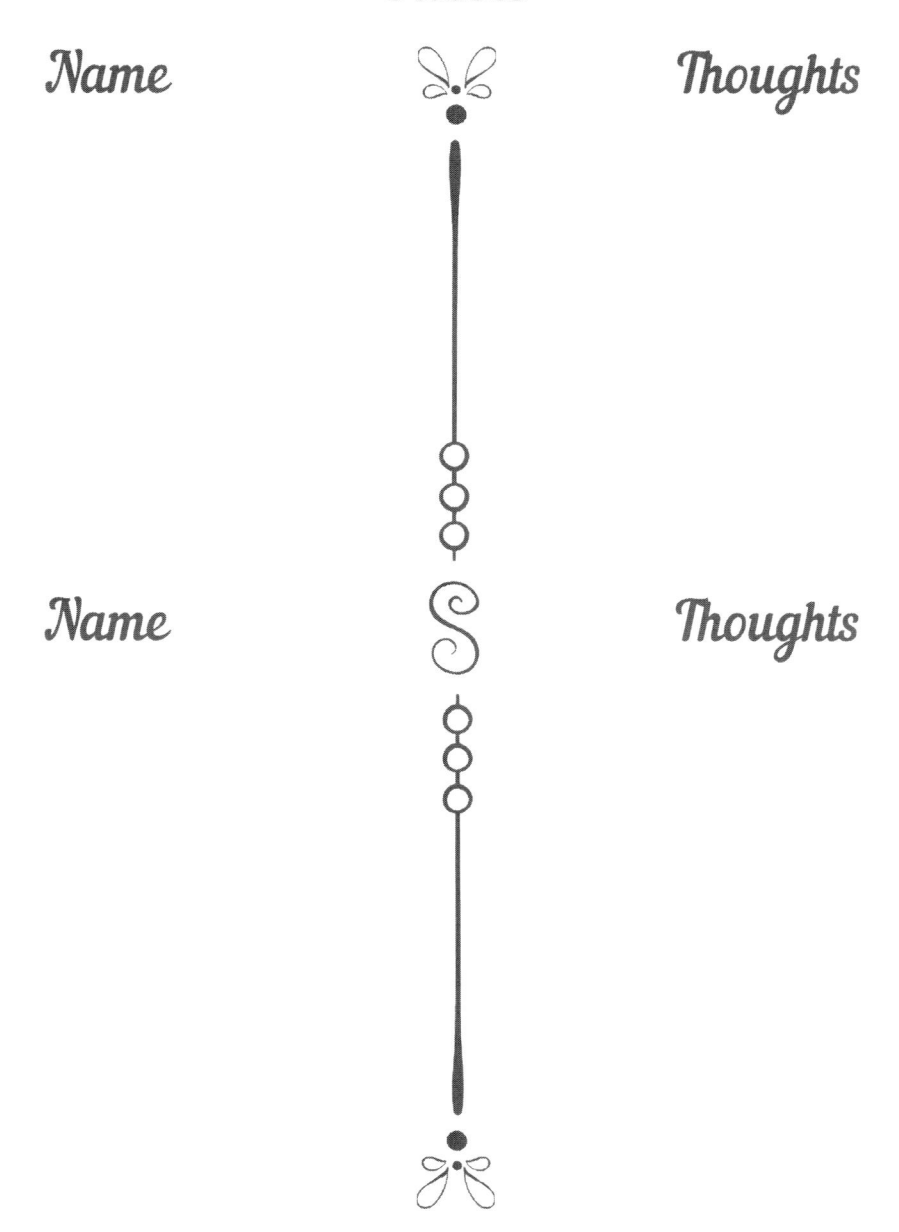

Name · Thoughts

Name · Thoughts

Guests

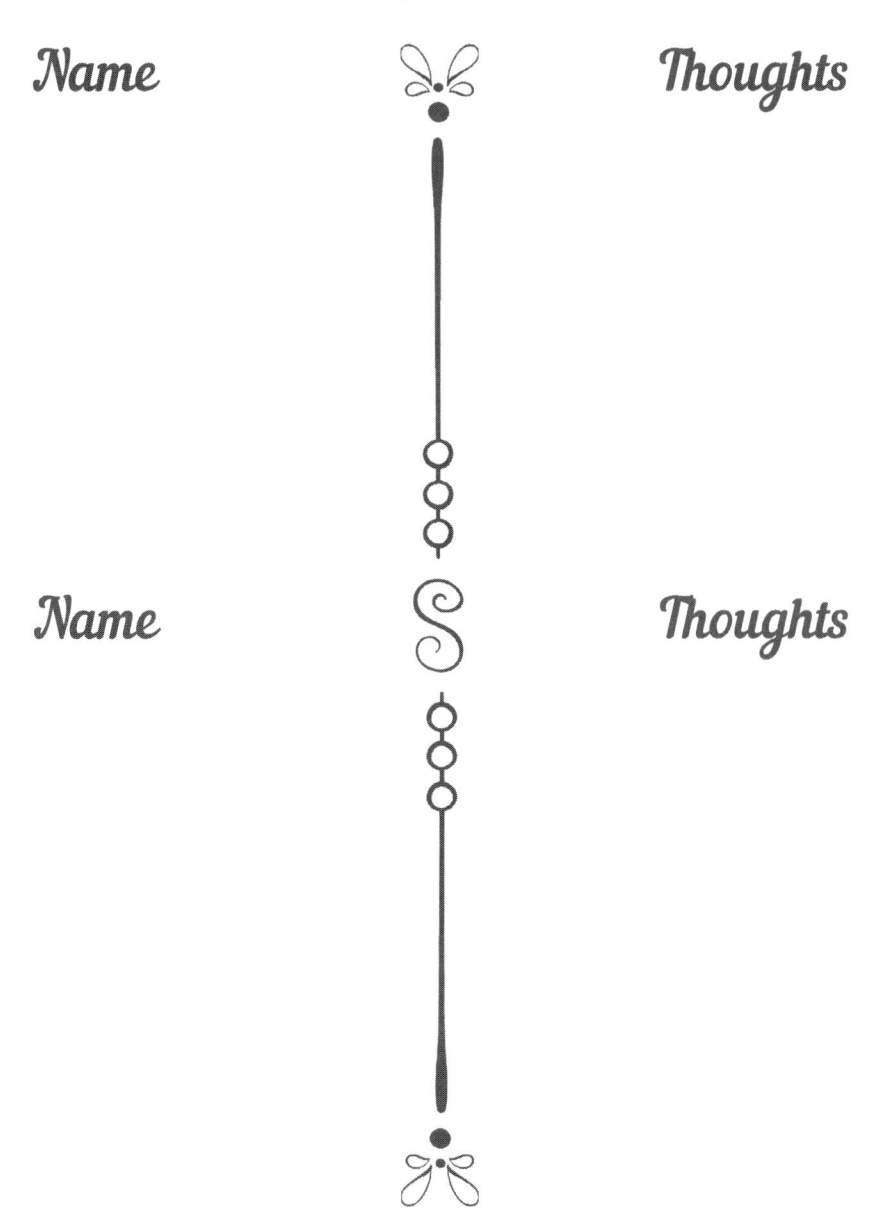

Name · Thoughts

Name · Thoughts

Guests

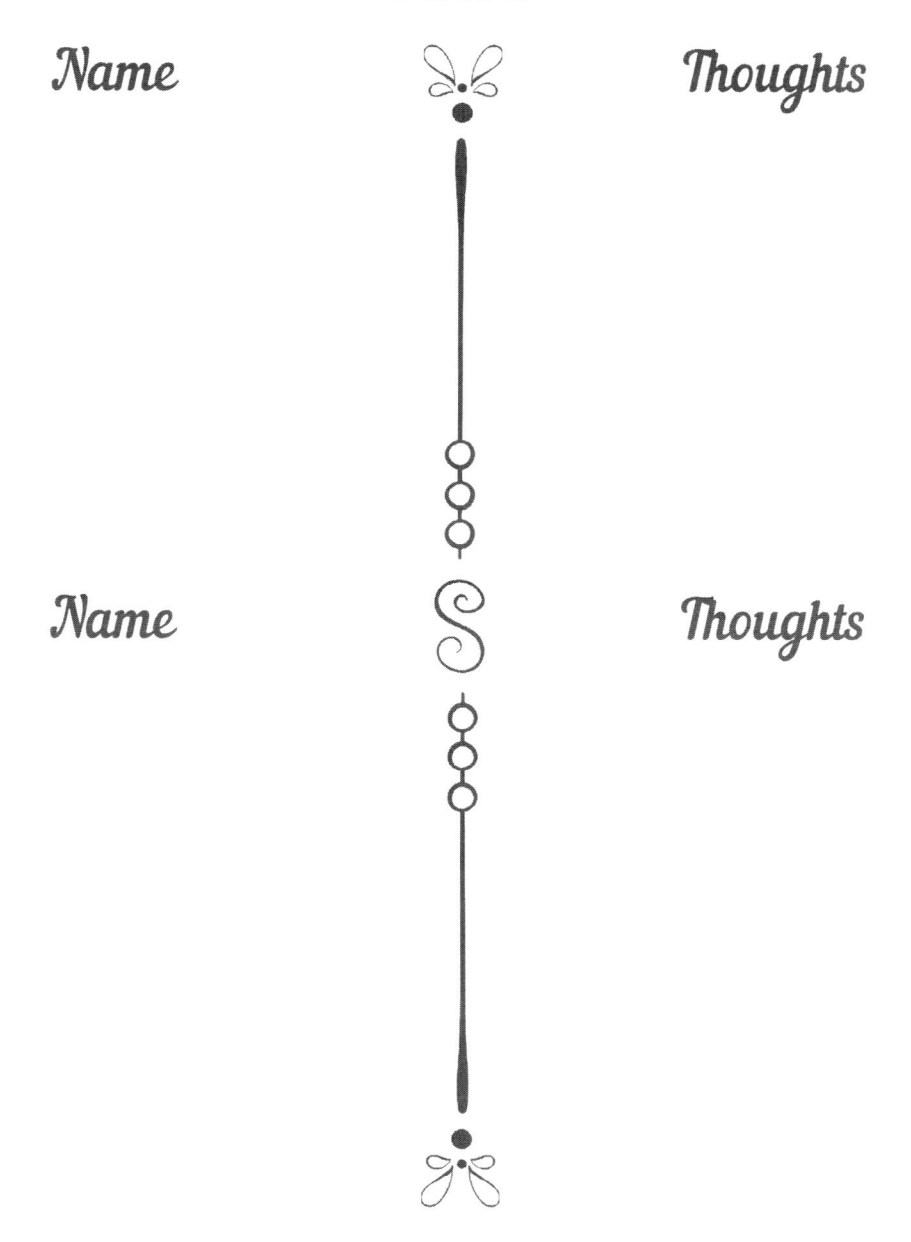

Name | Thoughts

Name | Thoughts

Guests

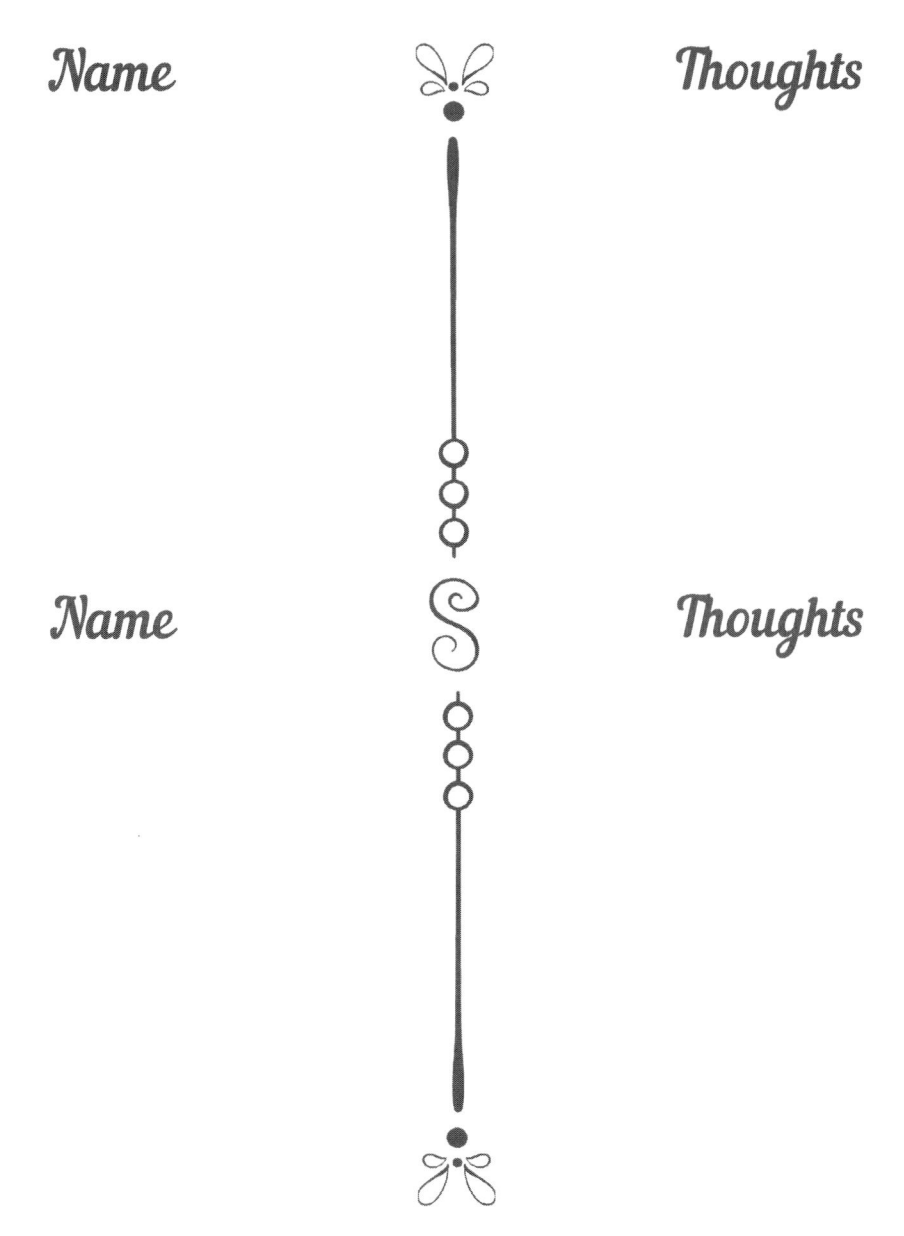

Name   *Thoughts*

Name   *Thoughts*

Guests

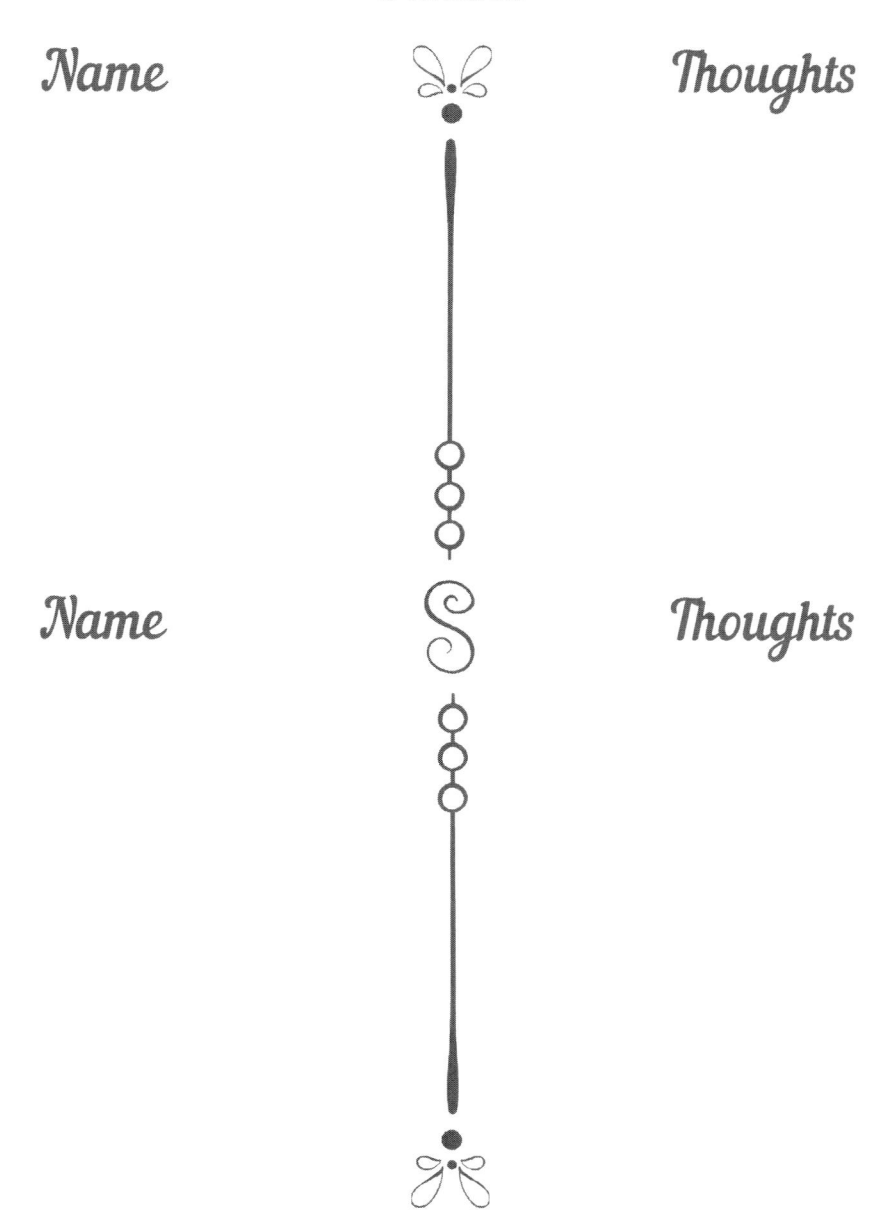

Name	Thoughts
Name	Thoughts

Guests

Name   Thoughts

Name   Thoughts

Guests

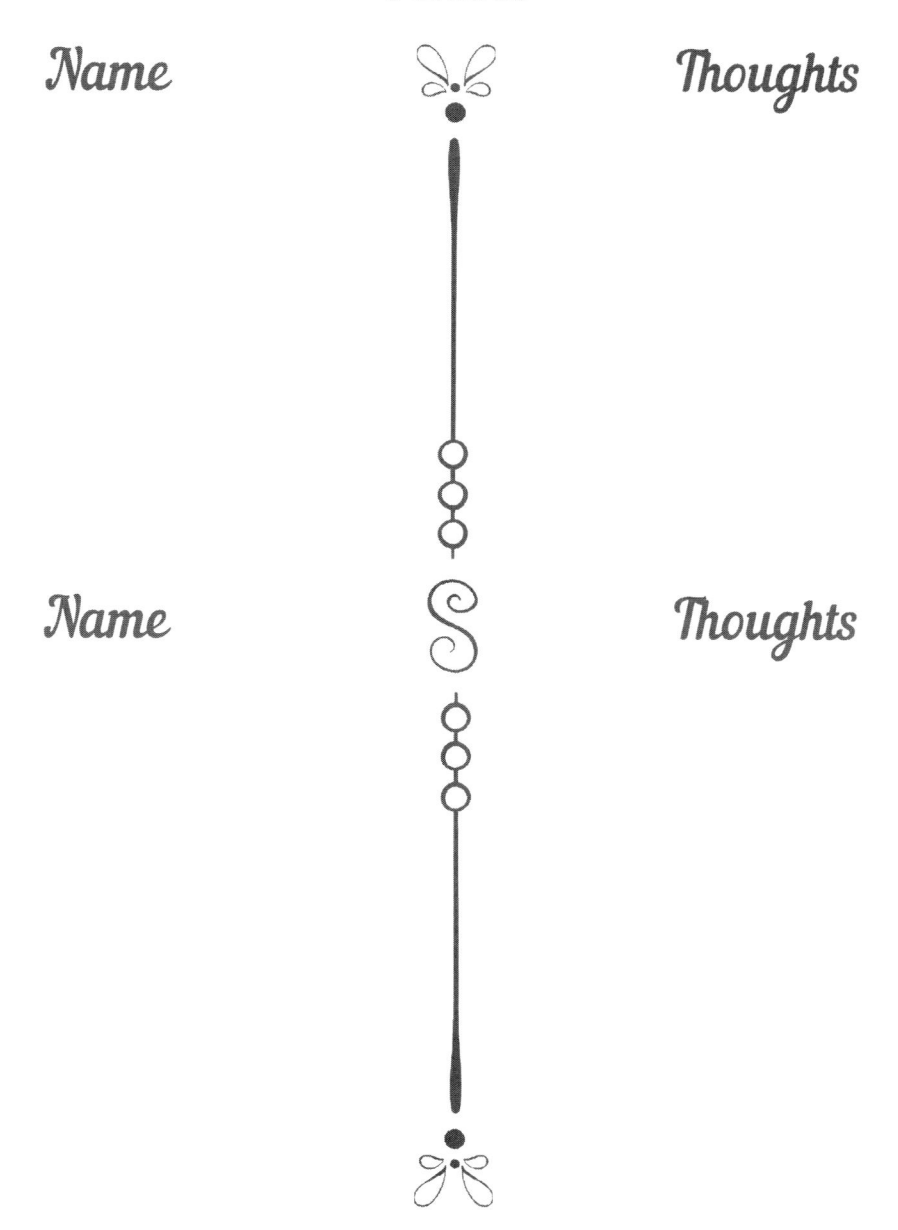

Name   *Thoughts*

Name   *Thoughts*

Guests

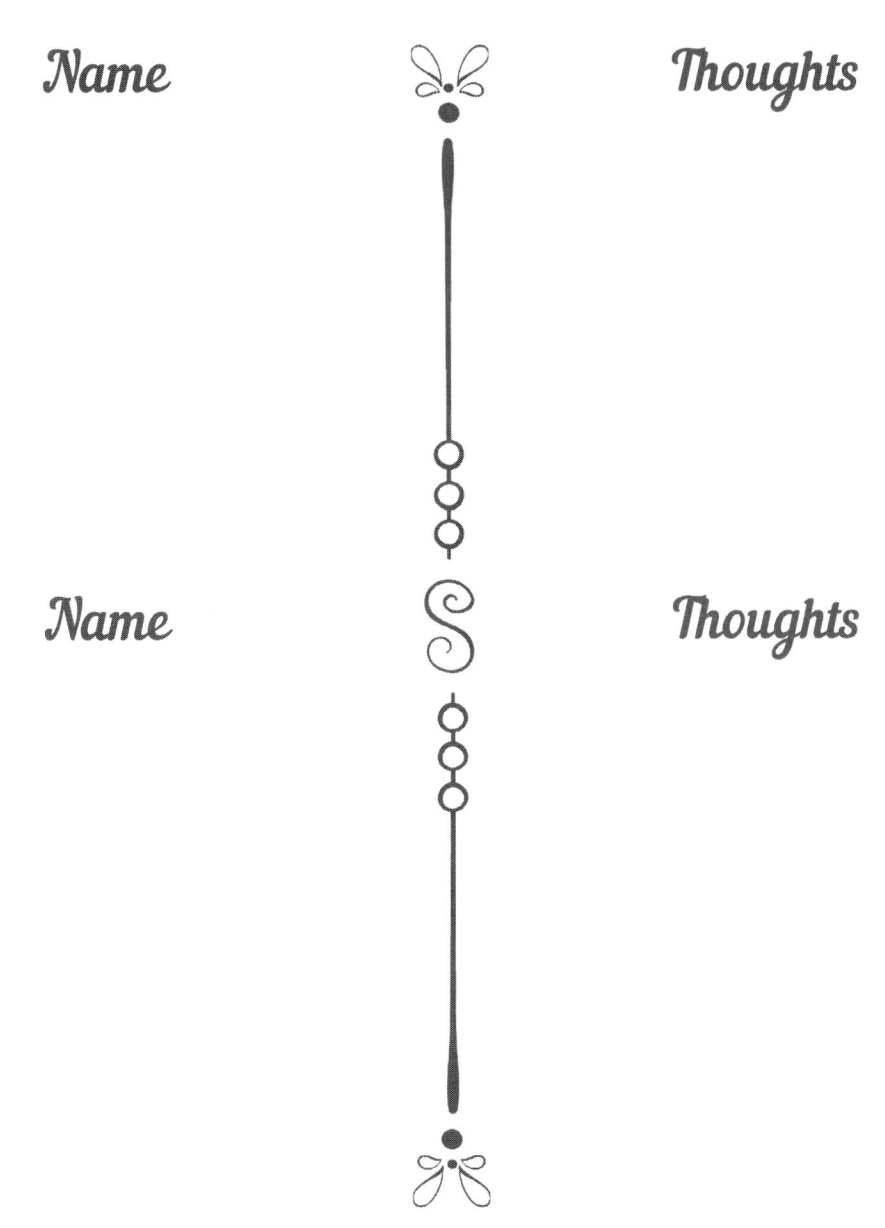

Name   Thoughts

Name   Thoughts

Guests

Name · Thoughts

Name · Thoughts

Guests

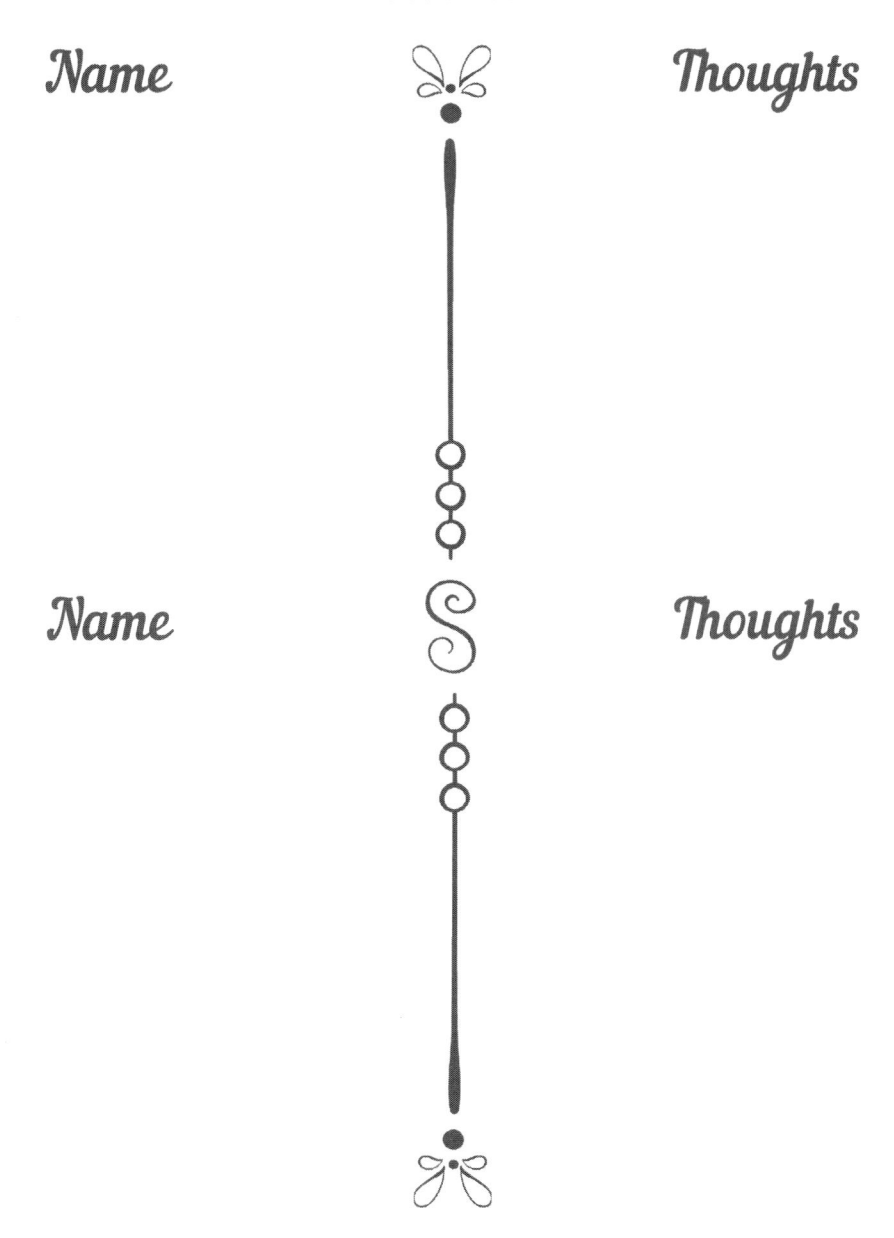

Name   *Thoughts*

Name   *Thoughts*

Guests

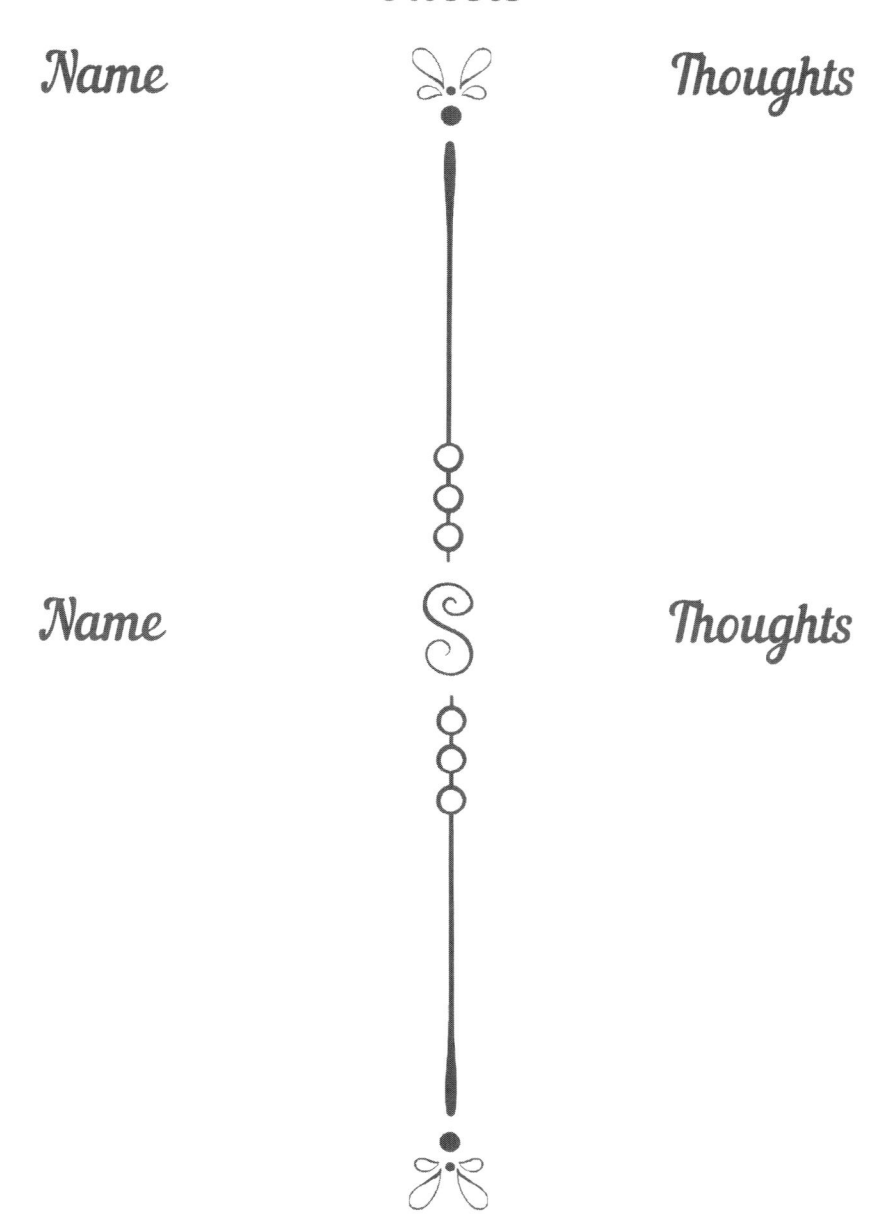

Name · Thoughts

Name · Thoughts

Guests

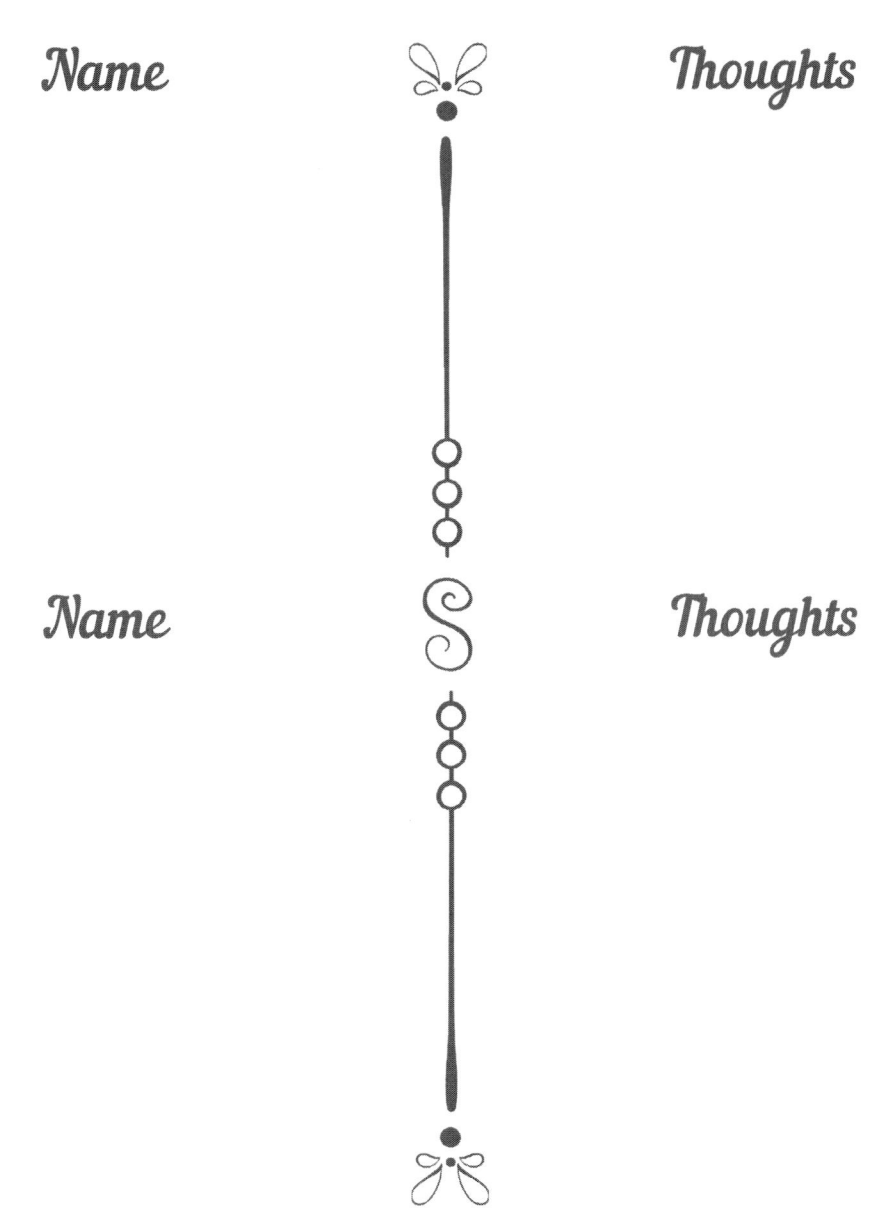

Name   *Thoughts*

Name   *Thoughts*

Guests

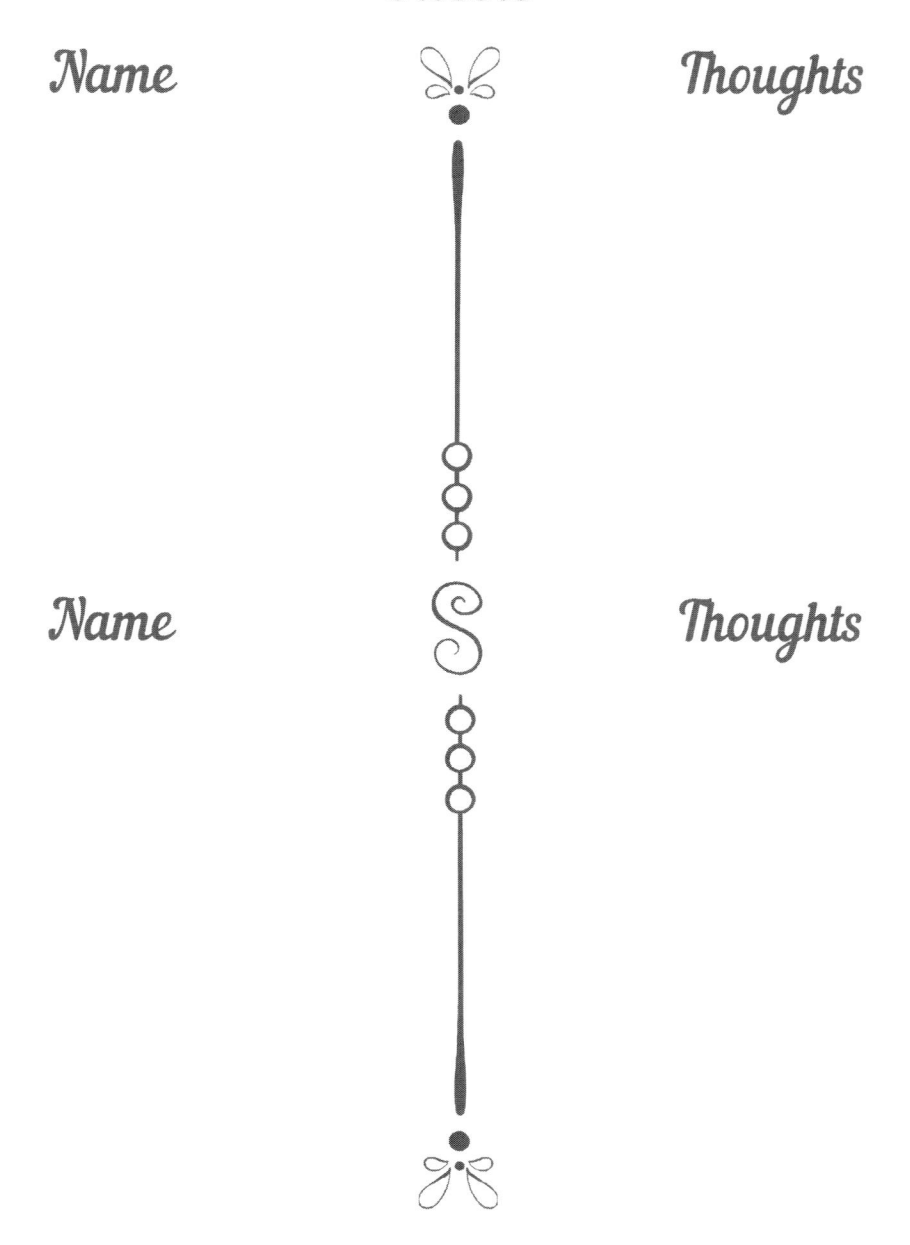

Name   Thoughts

Name   Thoughts

Guests

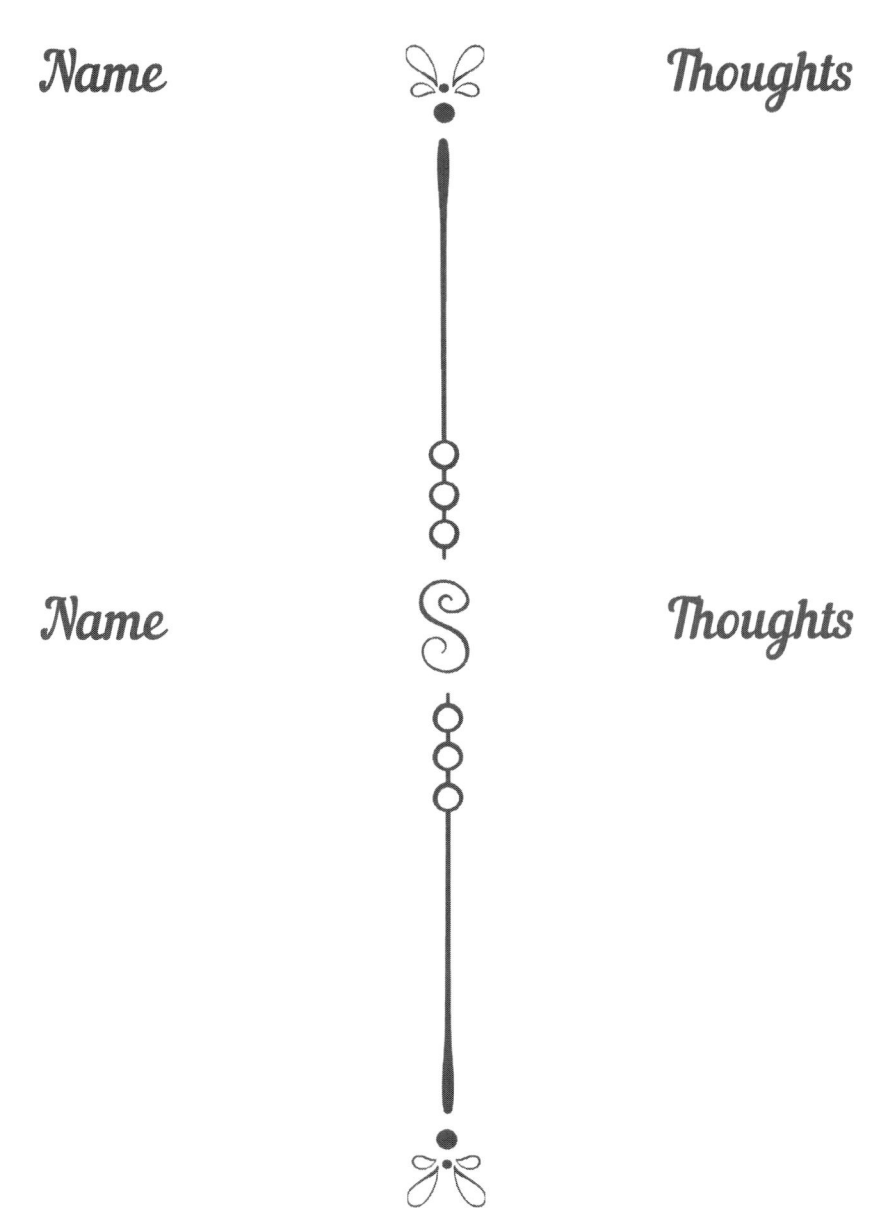

Name   Thoughts

Name   Thoughts

Guests

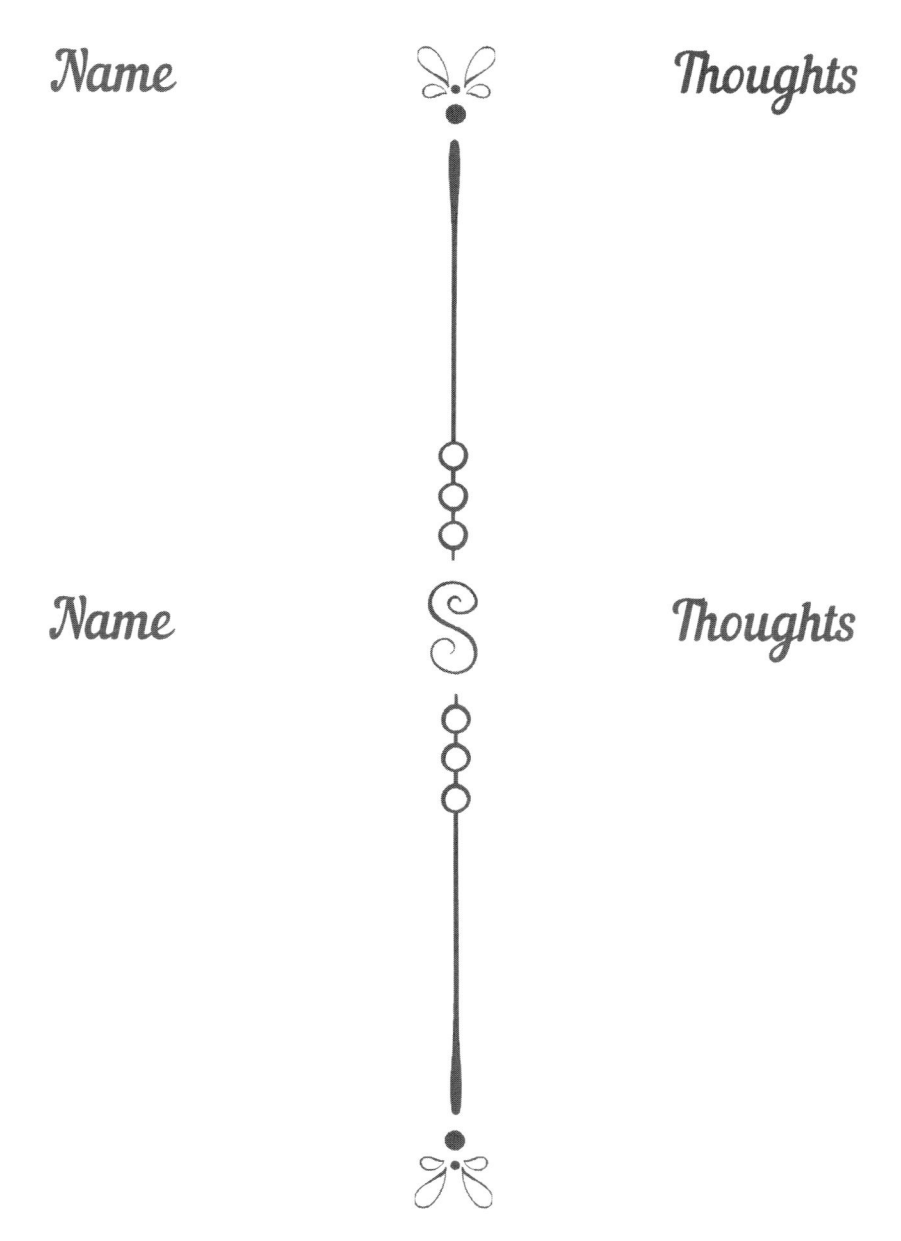

Name　　　　　　　　　Thoughts

Name　　　　　　　　　Thoughts

Guests

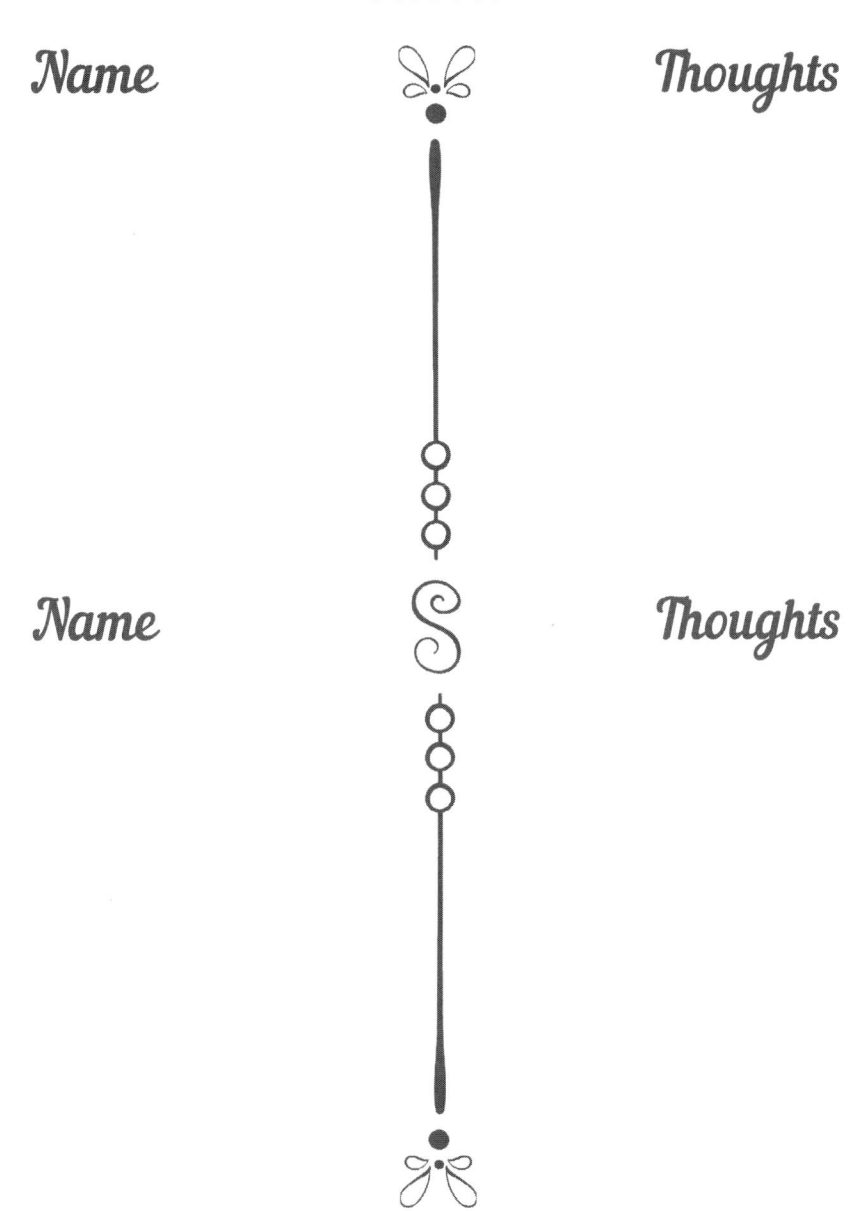

Name Thoughts

Name Thoughts

Guests

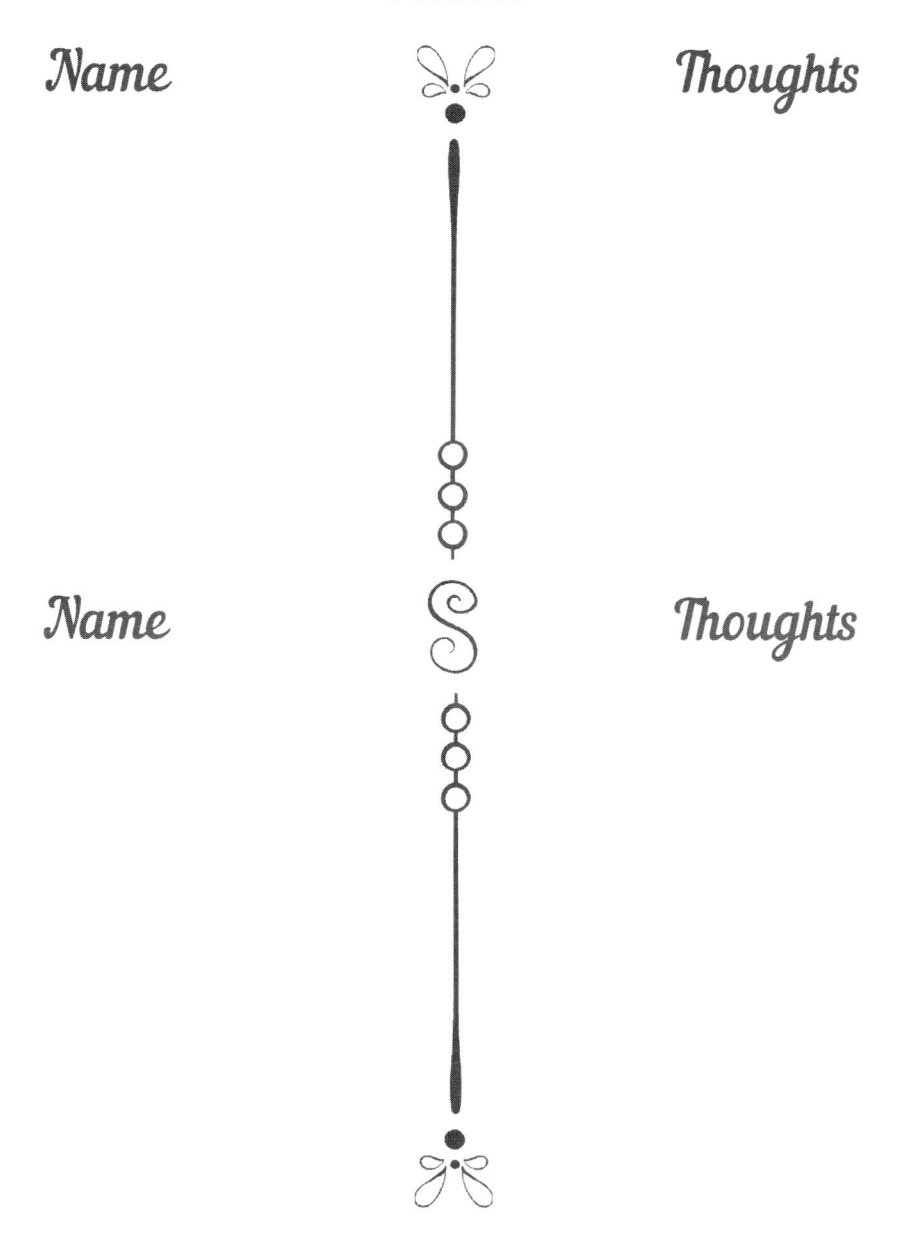

Name Thoughts

Name Thoughts

Guests

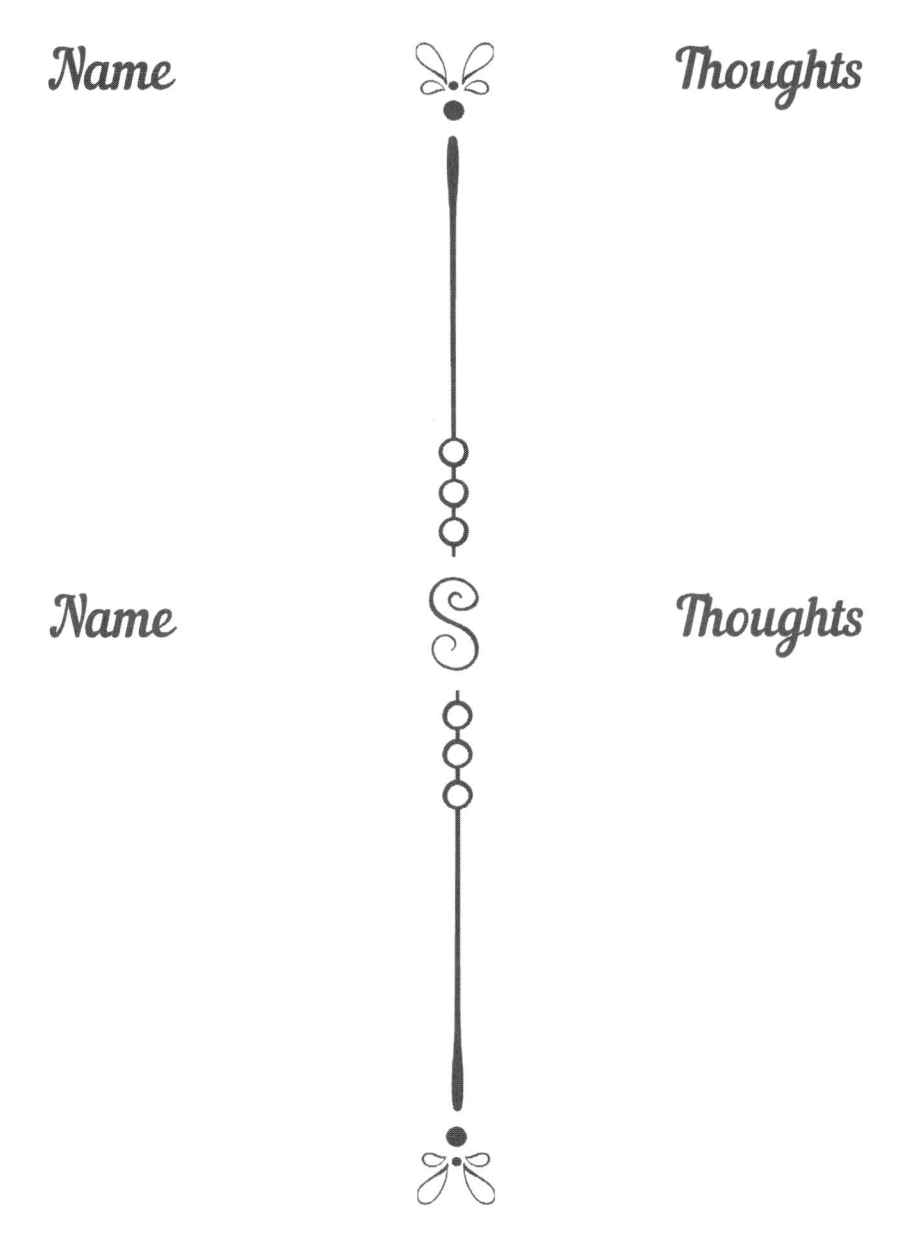

Name   *Thoughts*

Name   *Thoughts*

Guests

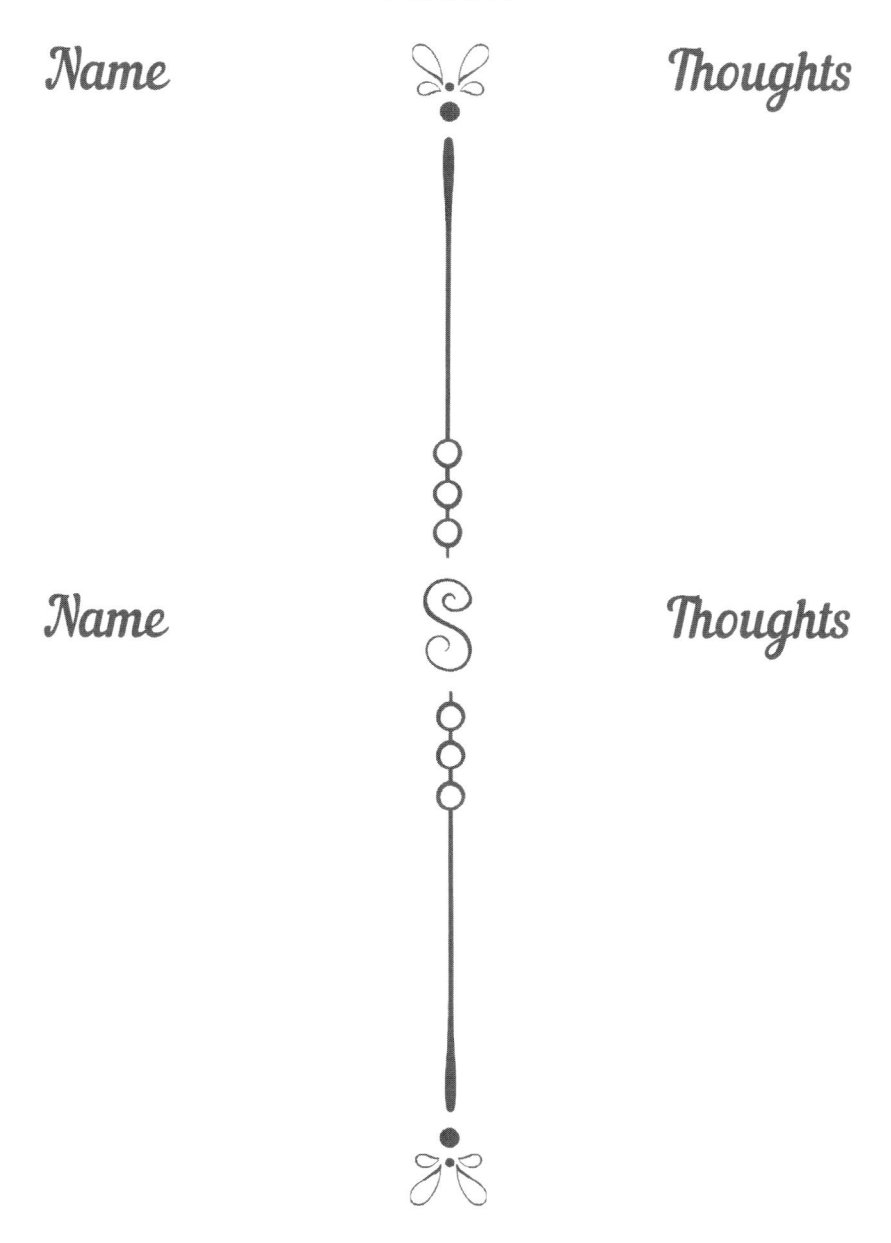

Name		Thoughts
Name	S	Thoughts

Guests

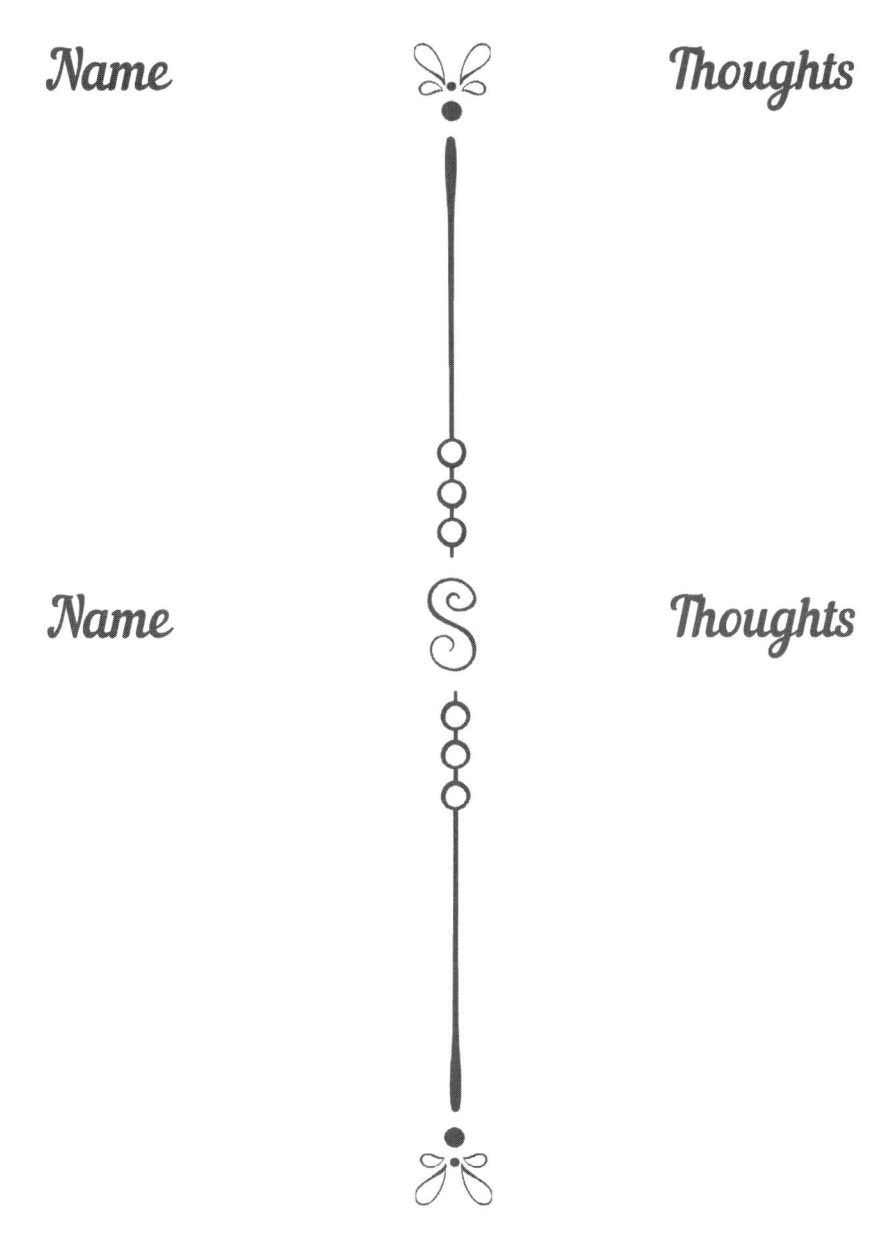

Name　　　　　　　　　　Thoughts

Name　　　　　　　　　　Thoughts

Guests

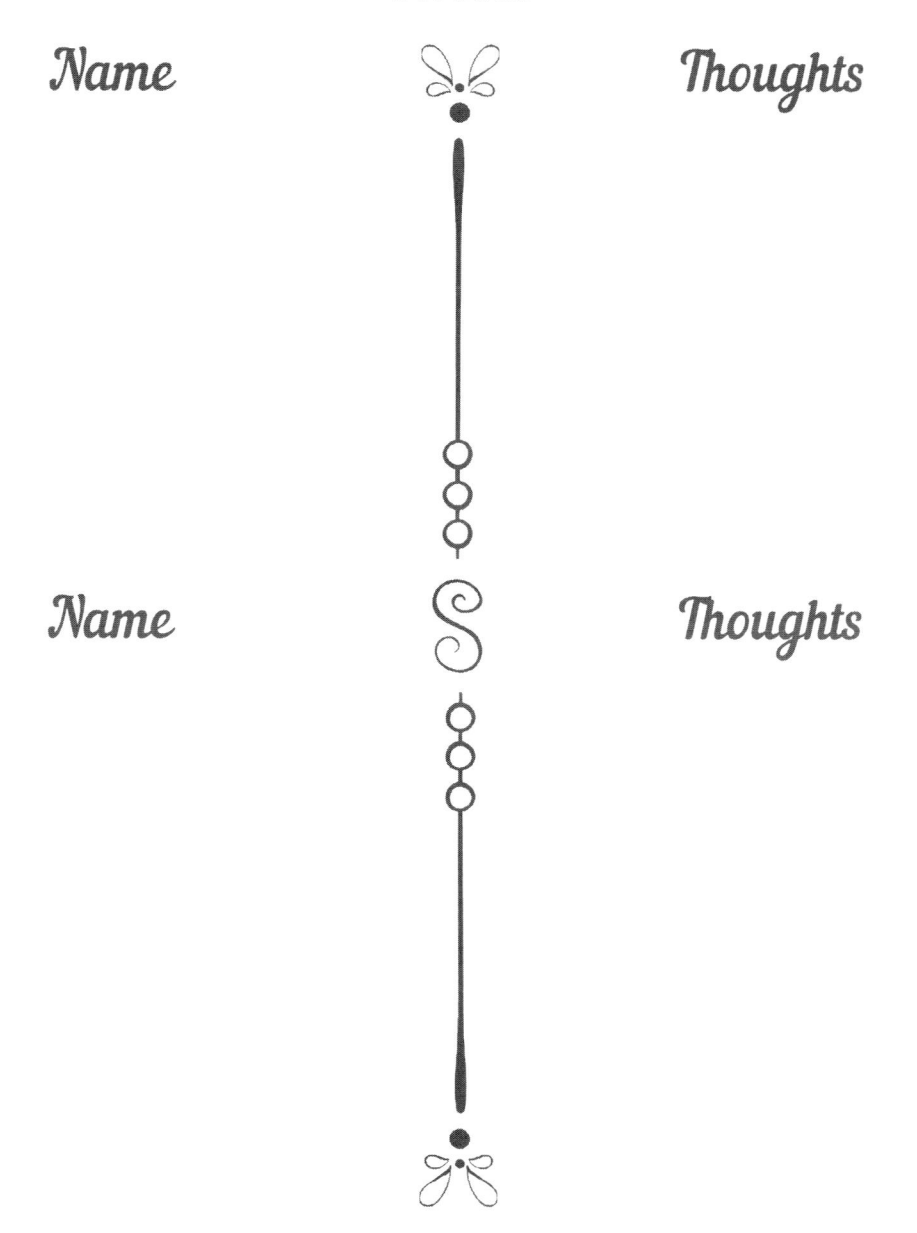

Name　　　　　　　　Thoughts

Name　　　　　　　　Thoughts

Guests

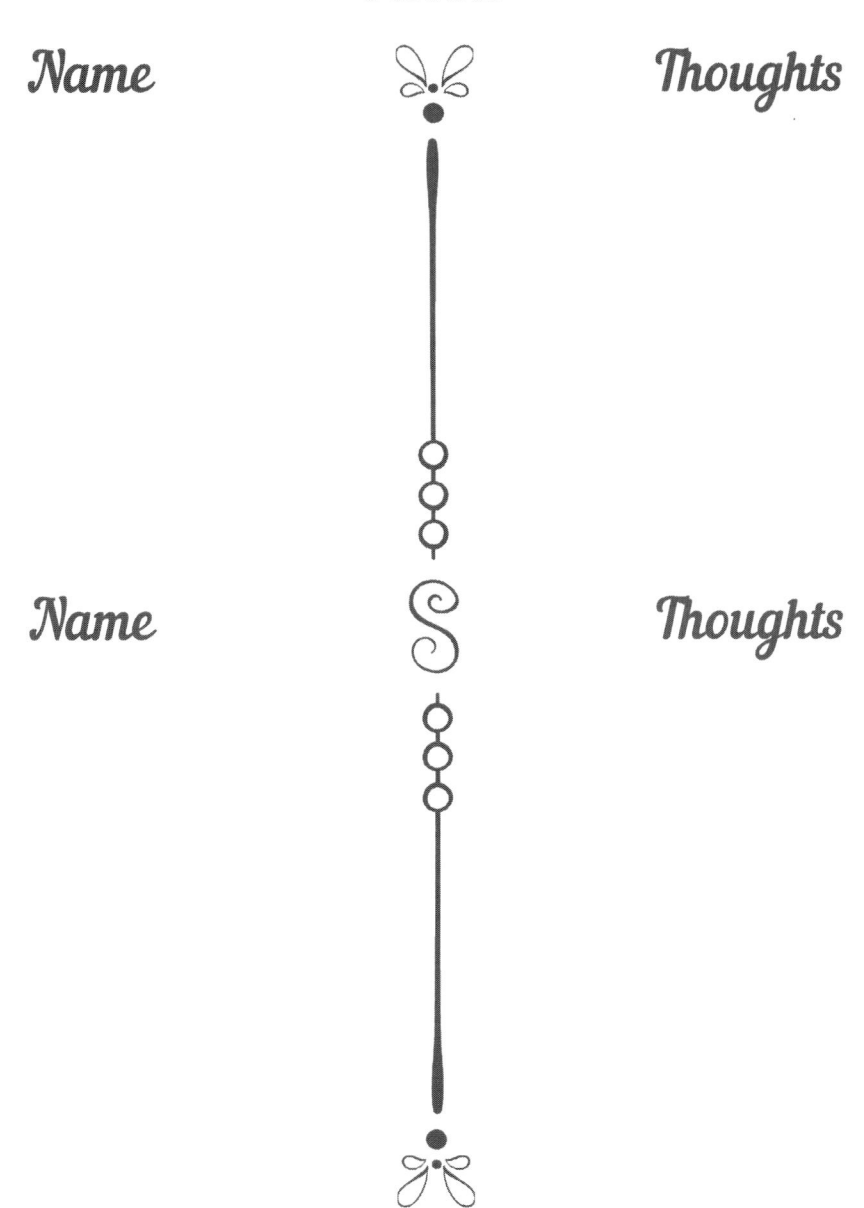

Name　　　　　　　　　　Thoughts

Name　　　　　　　　　　Thoughts

Guests

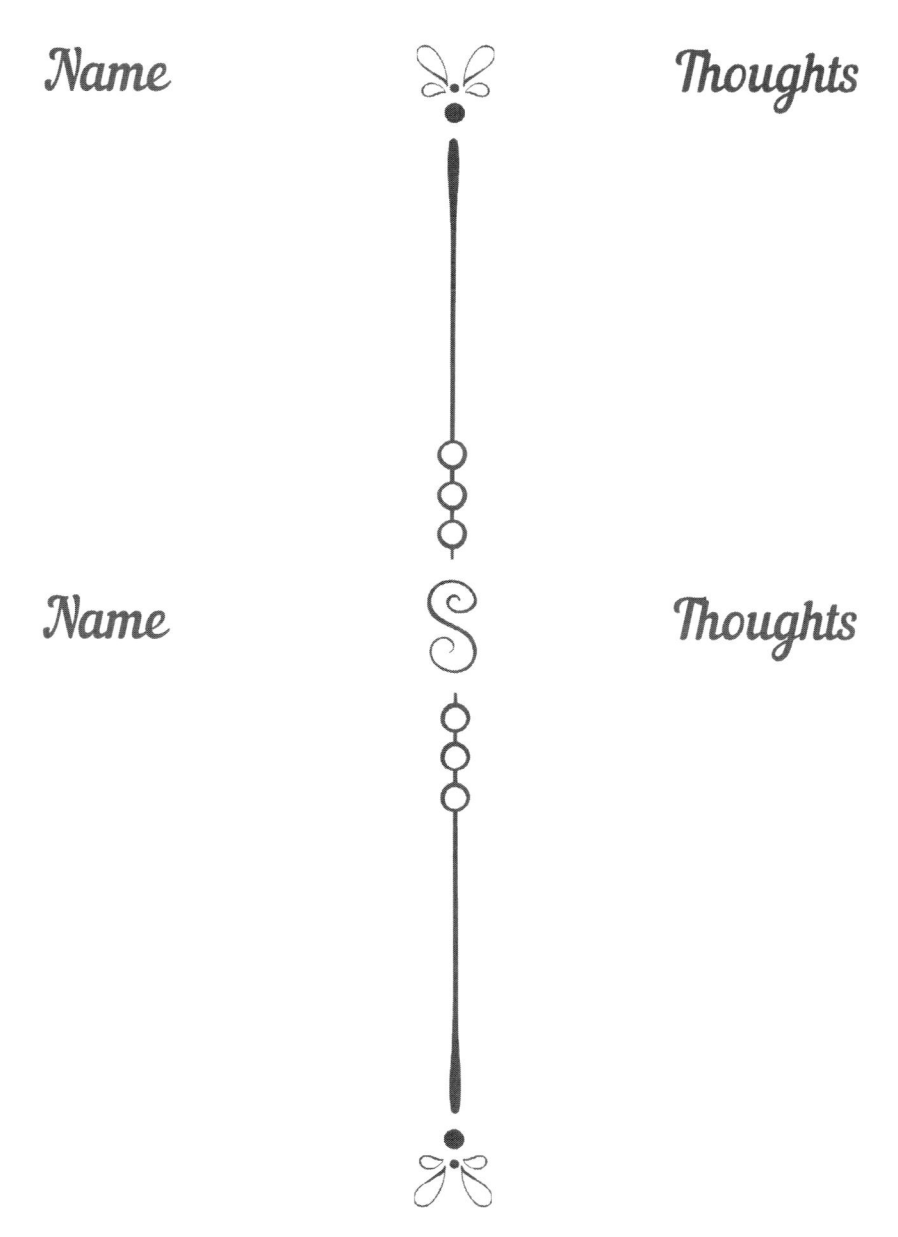

Name   Thoughts

Name   Thoughts

Guests

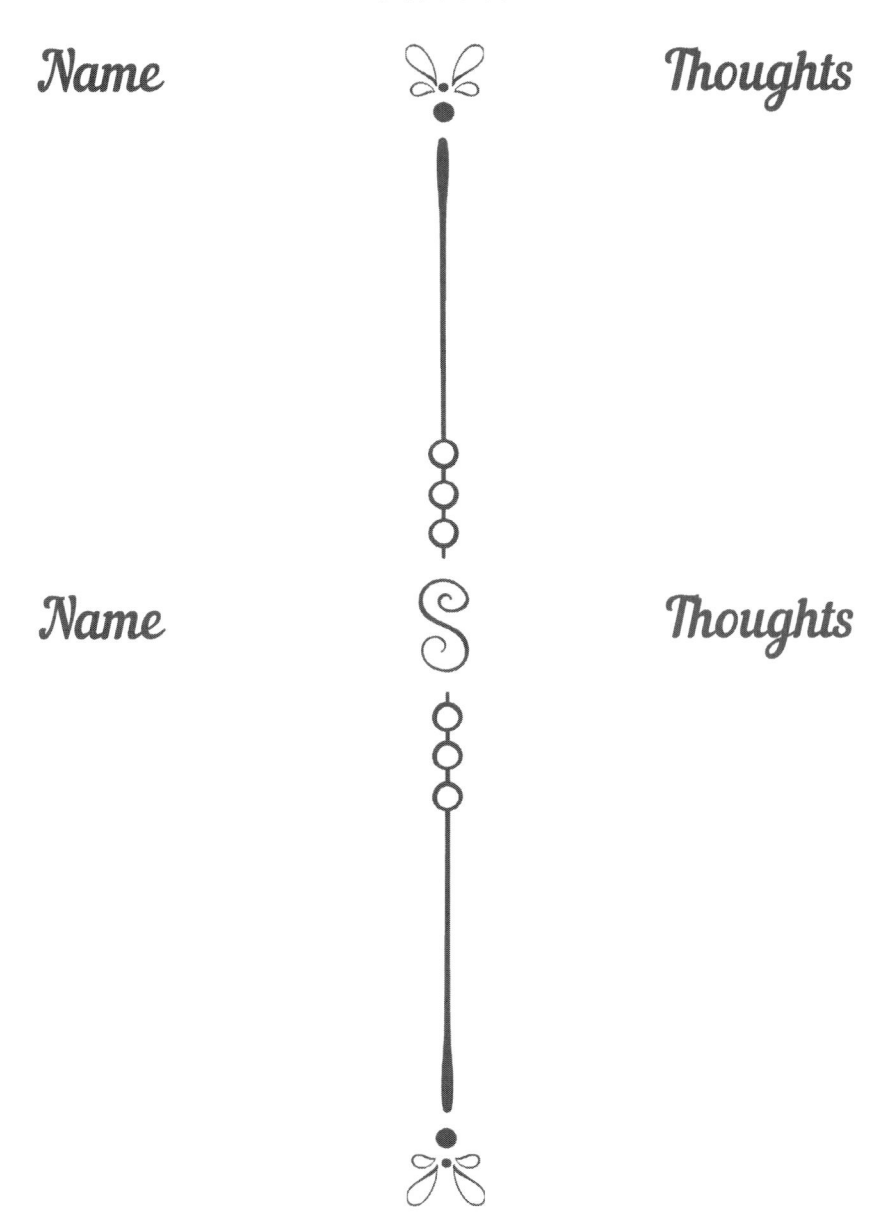

Name　　　　　　　　　　Thoughts

Name　　　　　　　　　　Thoughts

Guests

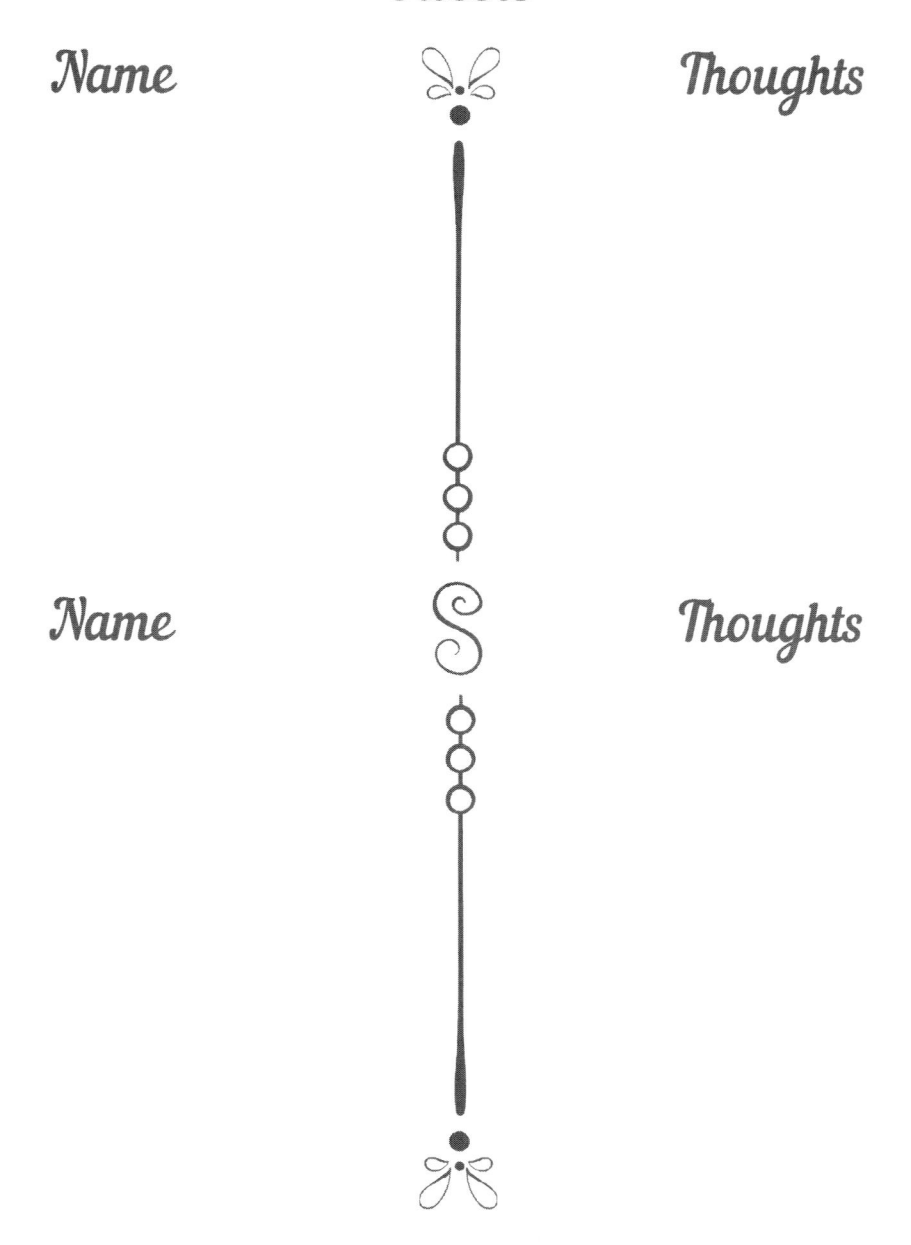

Name   Thoughts

Name   Thoughts

Guests

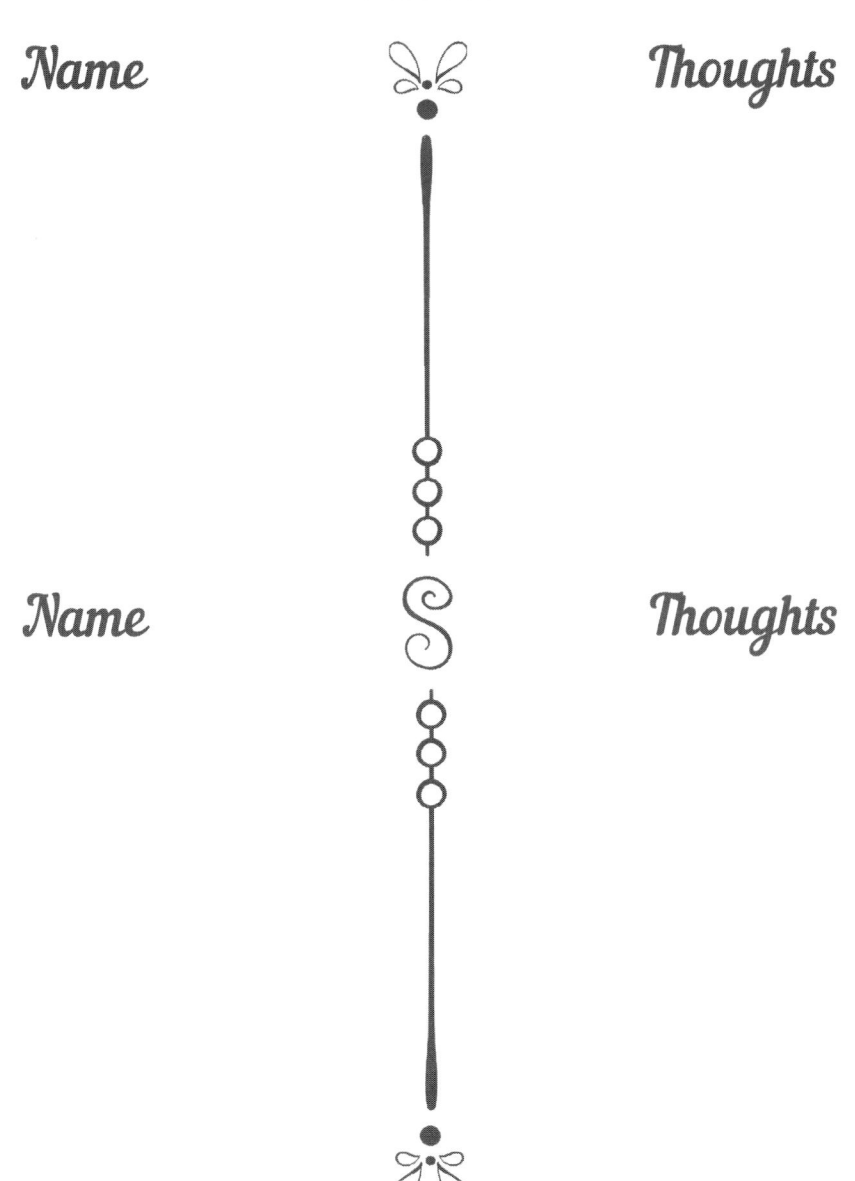

Name   *Thoughts*

Name   *Thoughts*

Guests

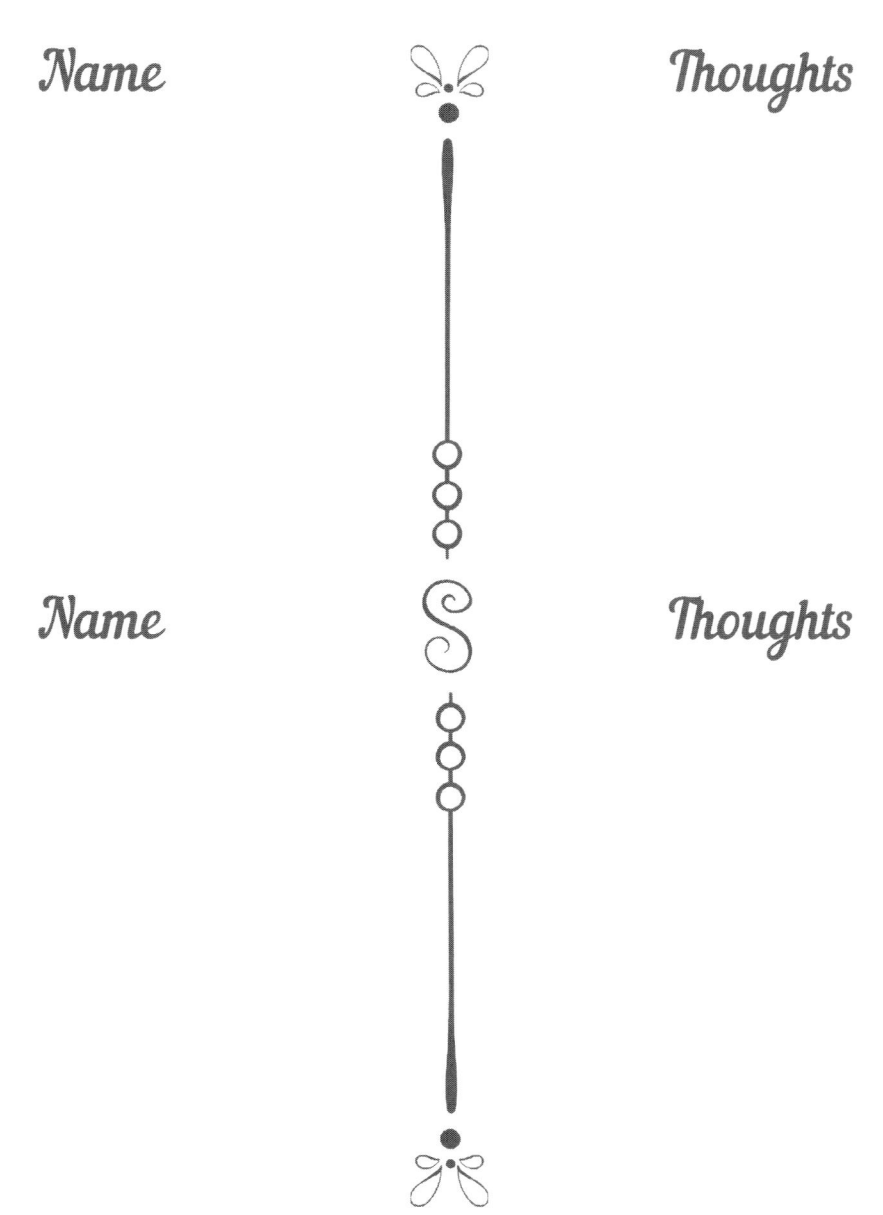

Name   Thoughts

Name   Thoughts

Guests

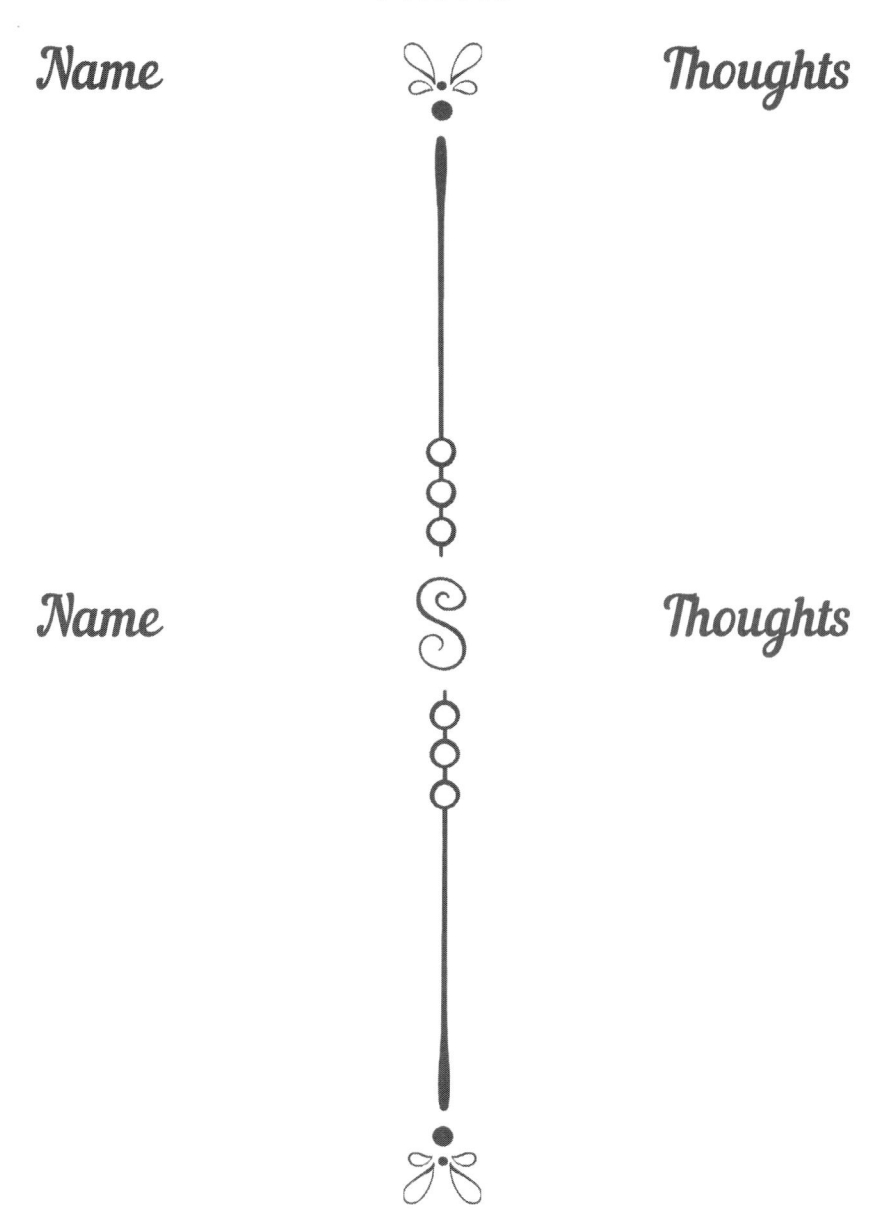

Name   Thoughts

Name   Thoughts

Guests

Name · Thoughts

Name · Thoughts

Guests

Name	Thoughts
Name	Thoughts

Guests

Name   Thoughts

Name   Thoughts

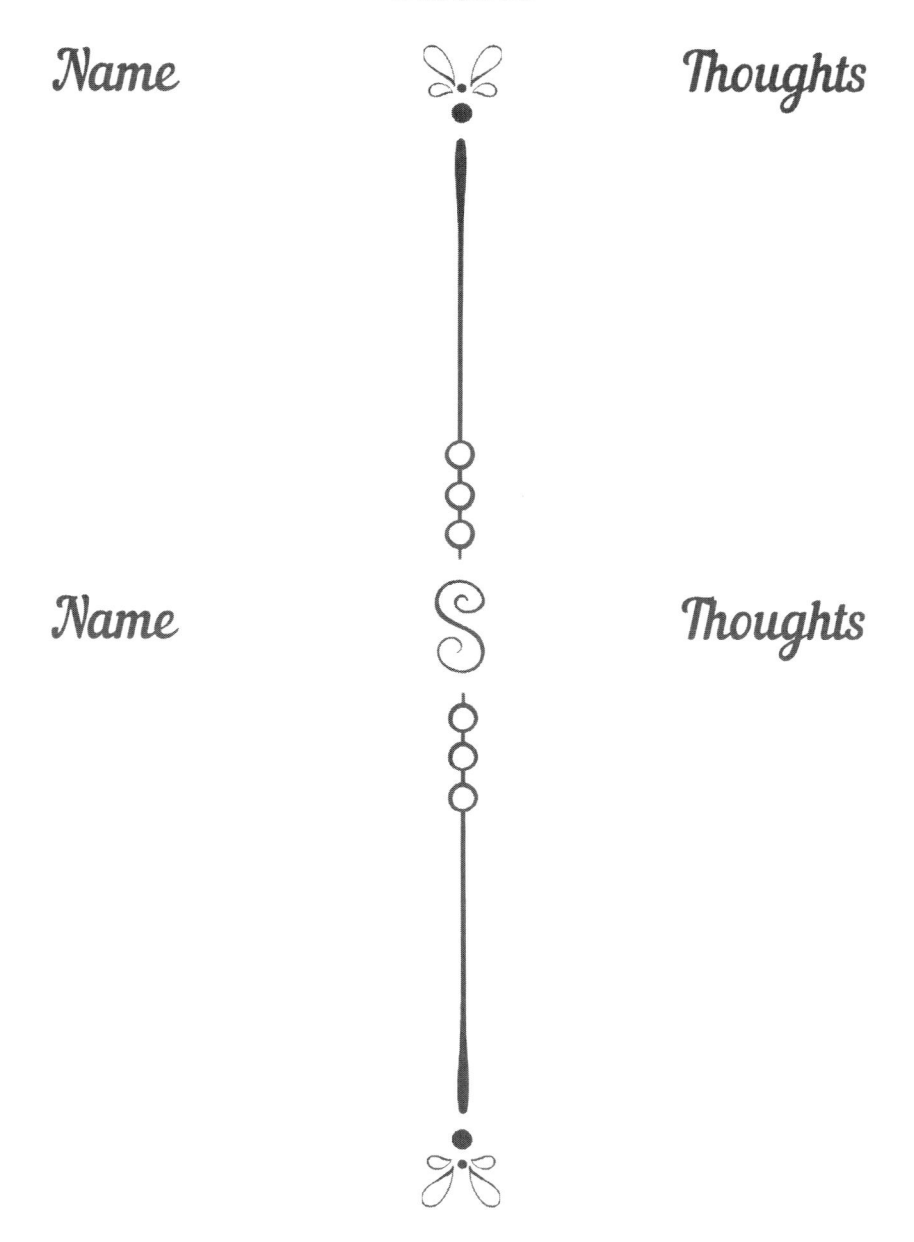

Guests

Name　　　　　　　　　　Thoughts

Name　　　　　　　　　　Thoughts

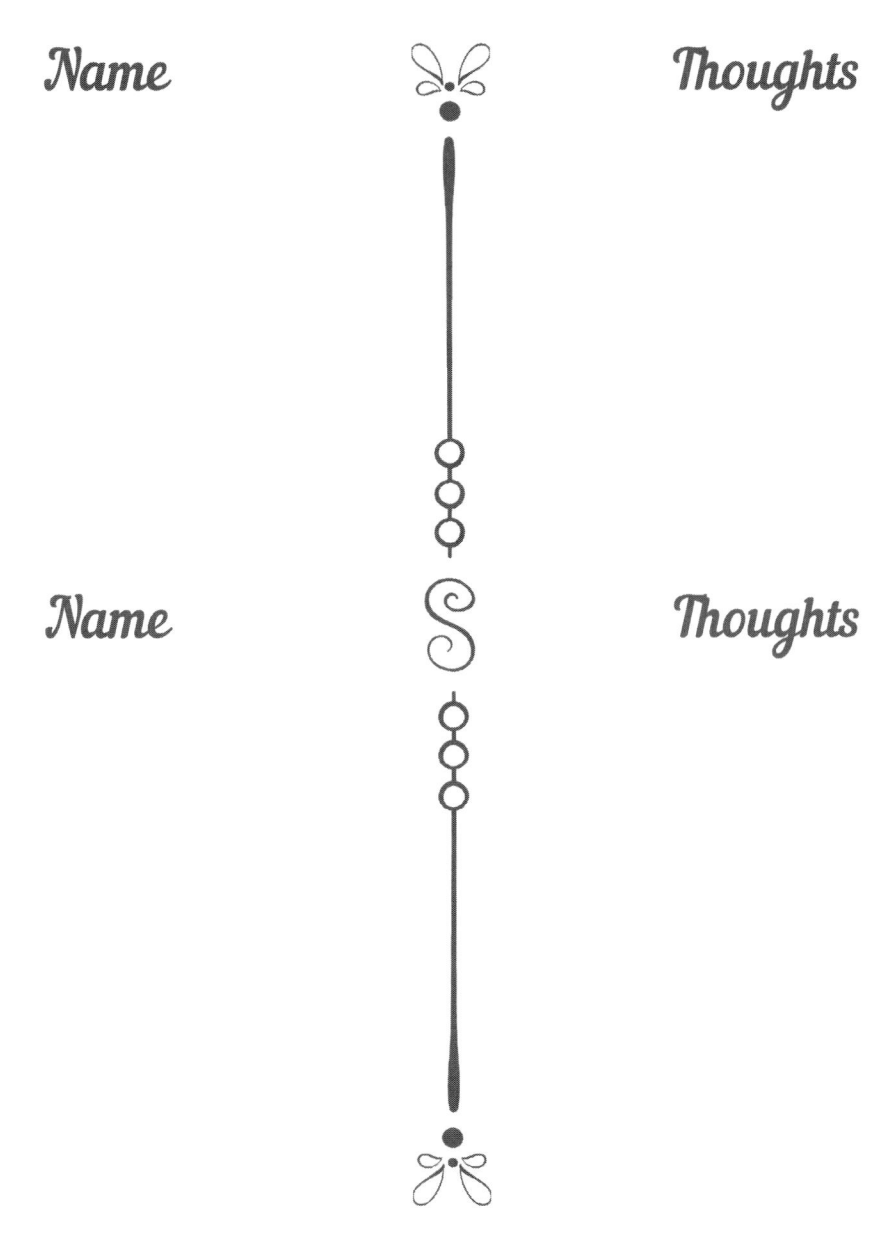

Guests

Name · · · Thoughts

Name · · · Thoughts

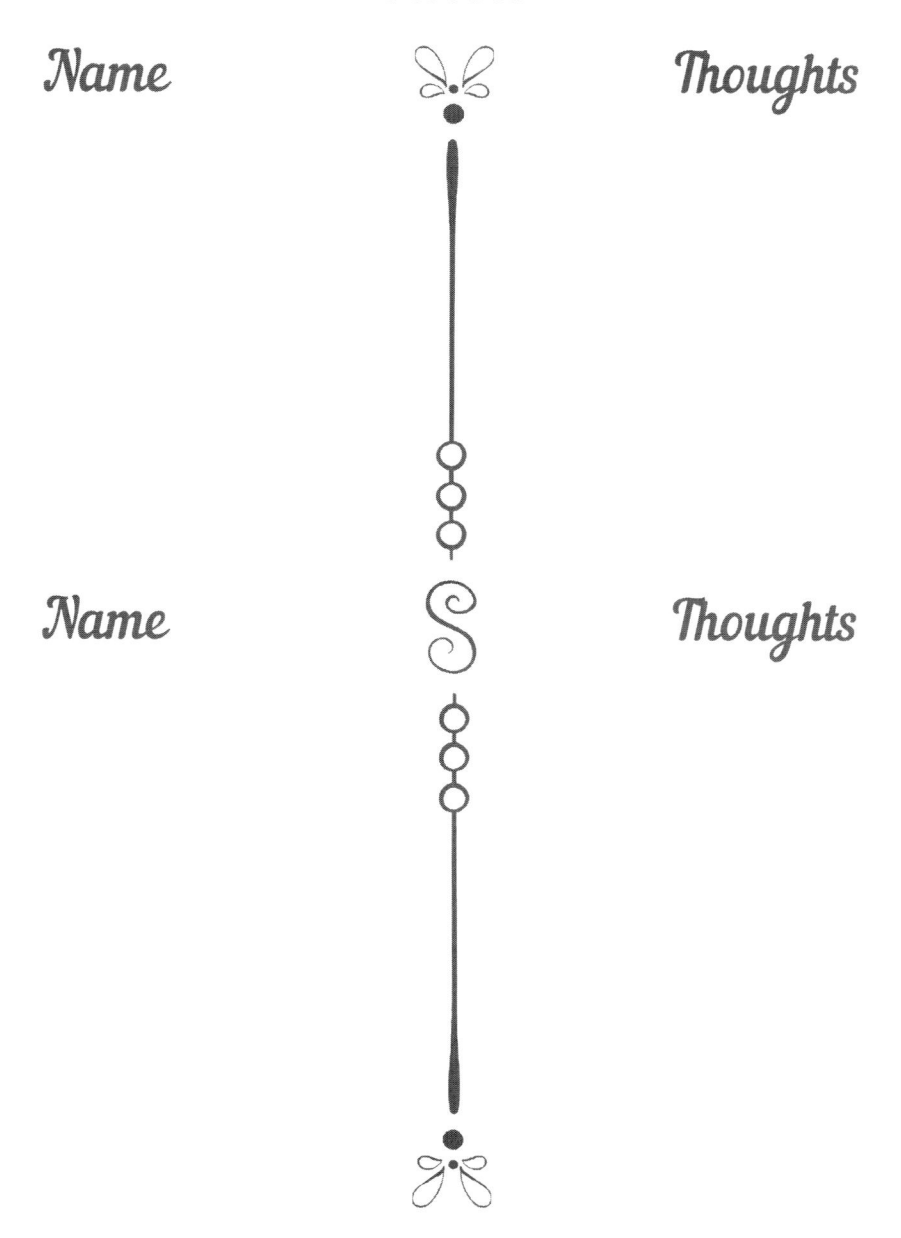

Guests

Name   *Thoughts*

Name   *Thoughts*

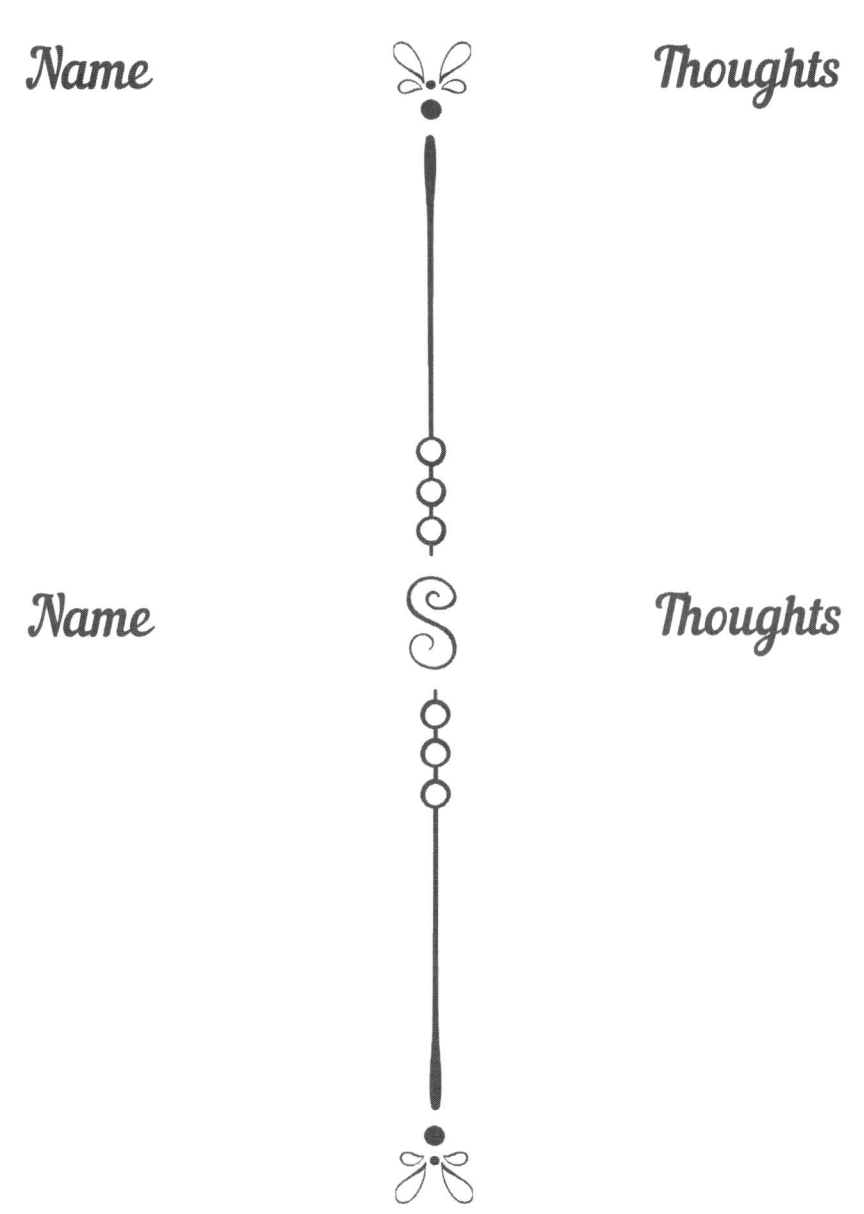

Guests

Name   *Thoughts*

Name   *Thoughts*

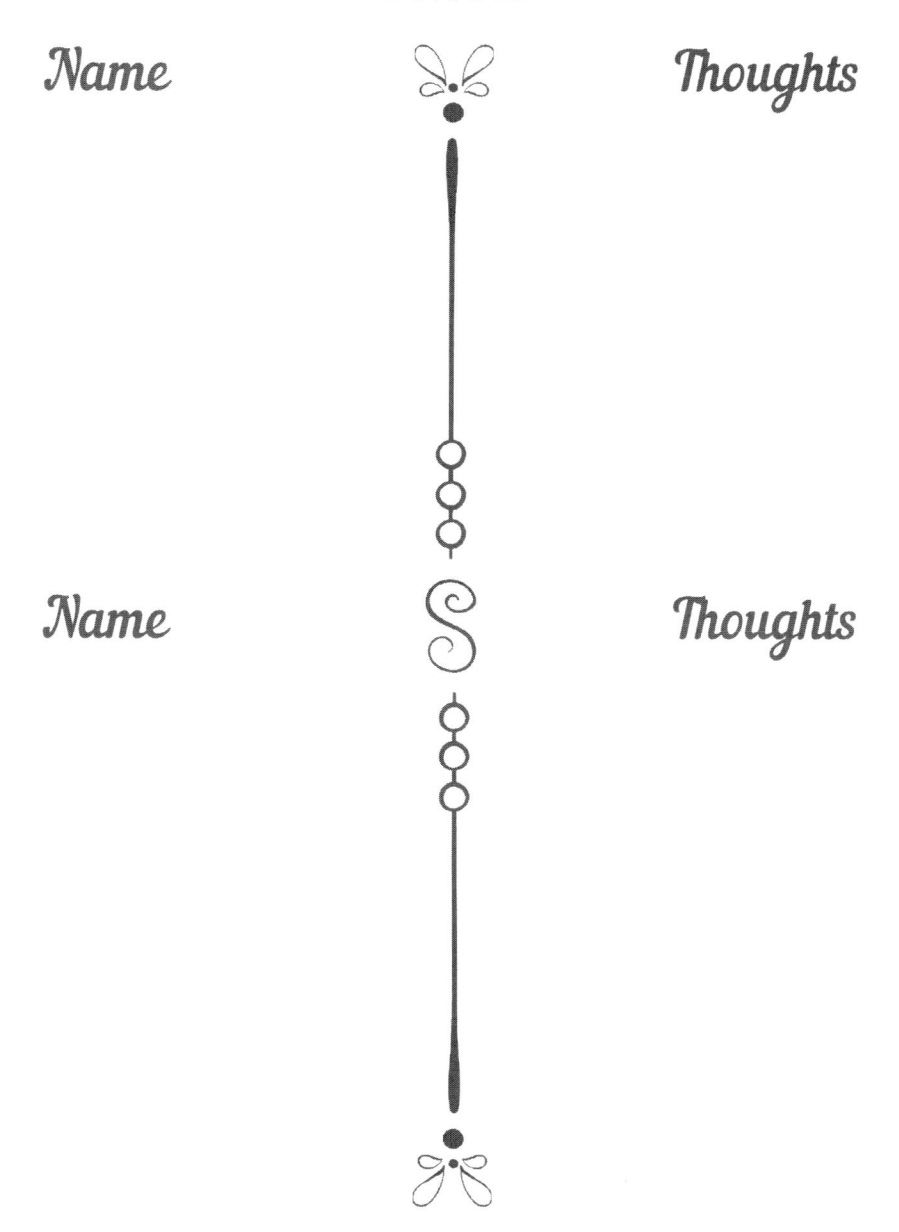

Guests

Name　　　　　　　　　　　Thoughts

Name　　　　　　　　　　　Thoughts

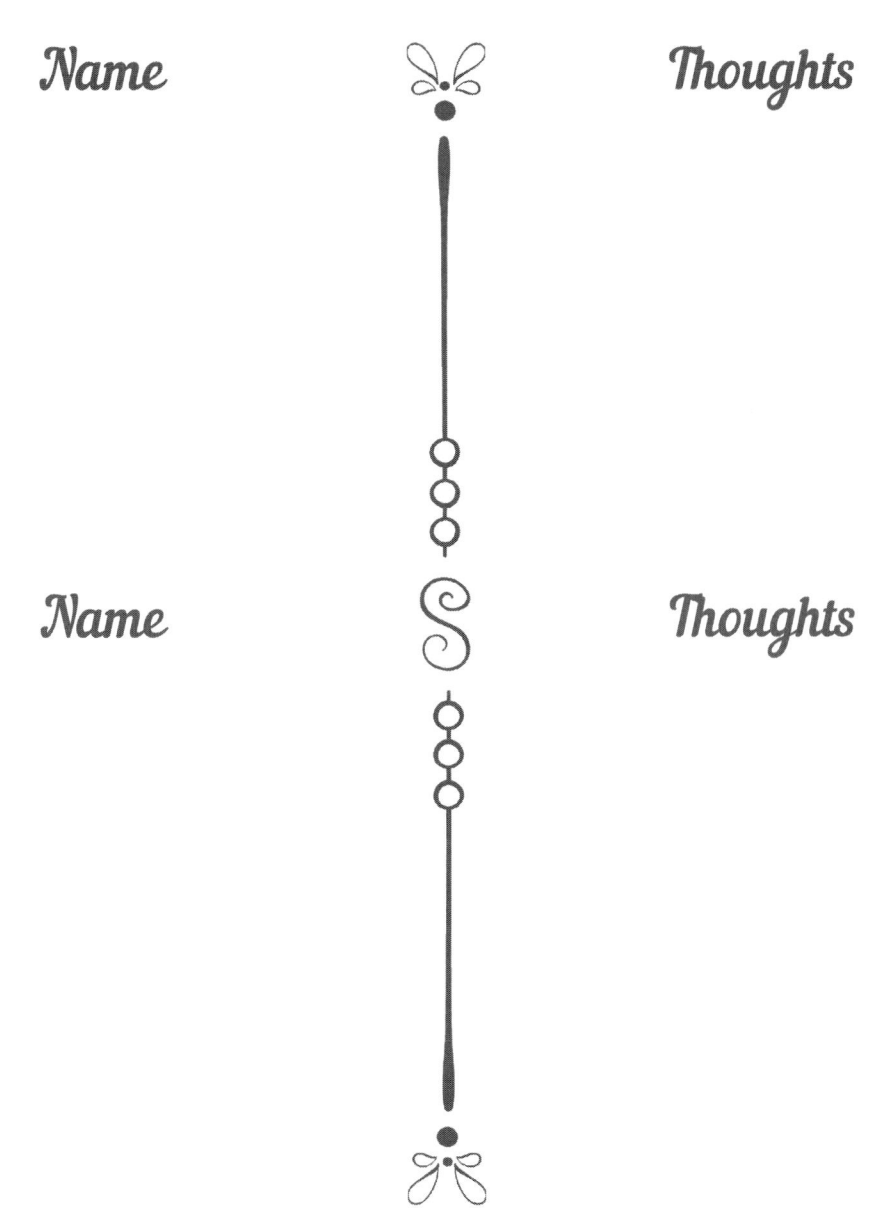

Guests

Name   Thoughts

Name   Thoughts

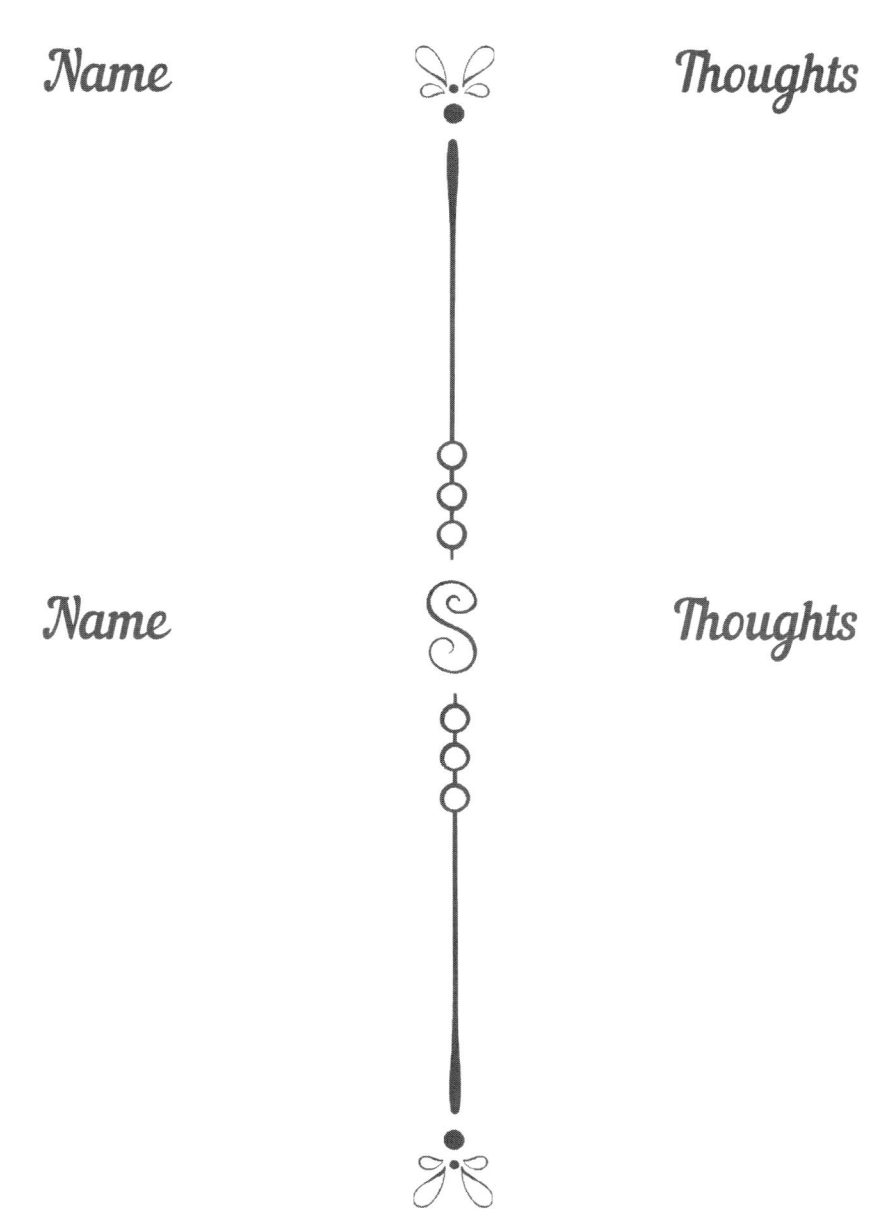

Guests

Name   Thoughts

Name   Thoughts

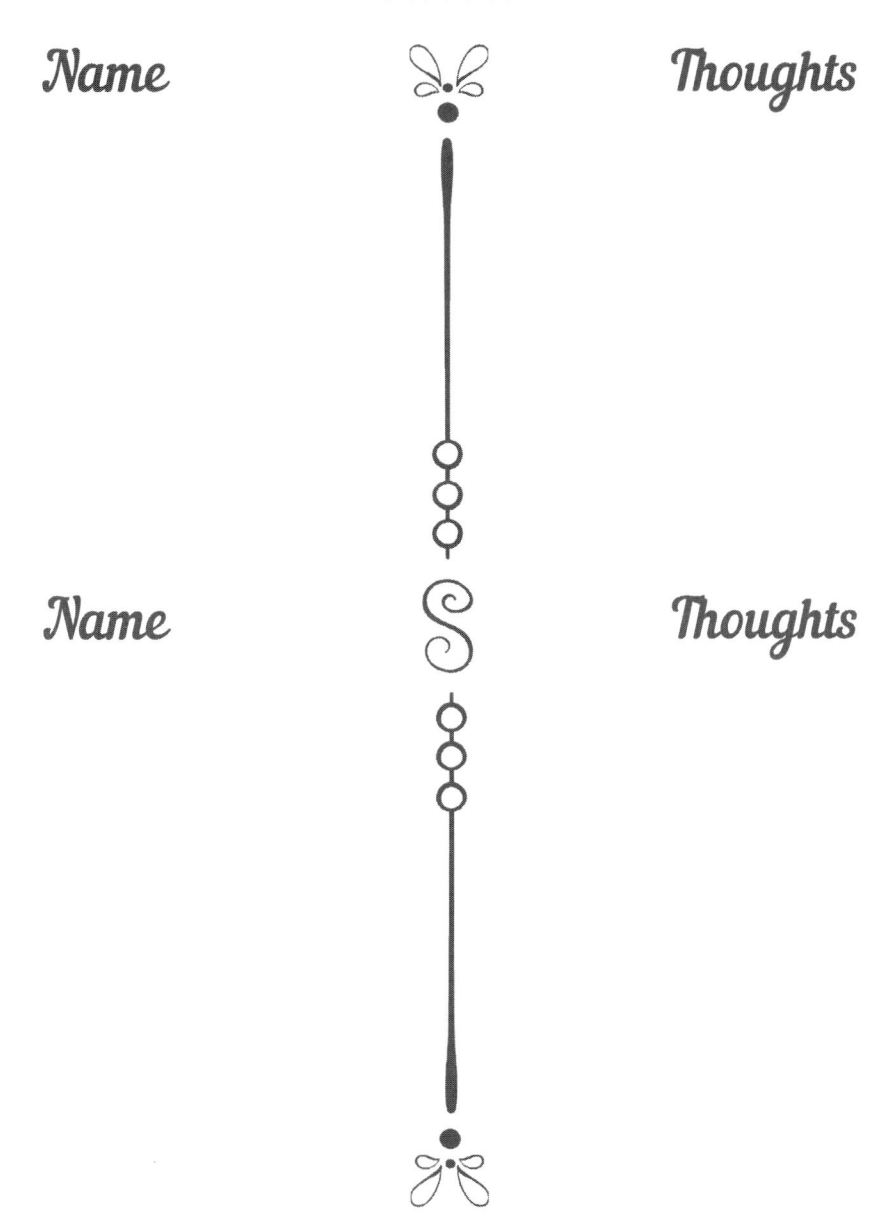

Guests

Name · Thoughts

Name · Thoughts

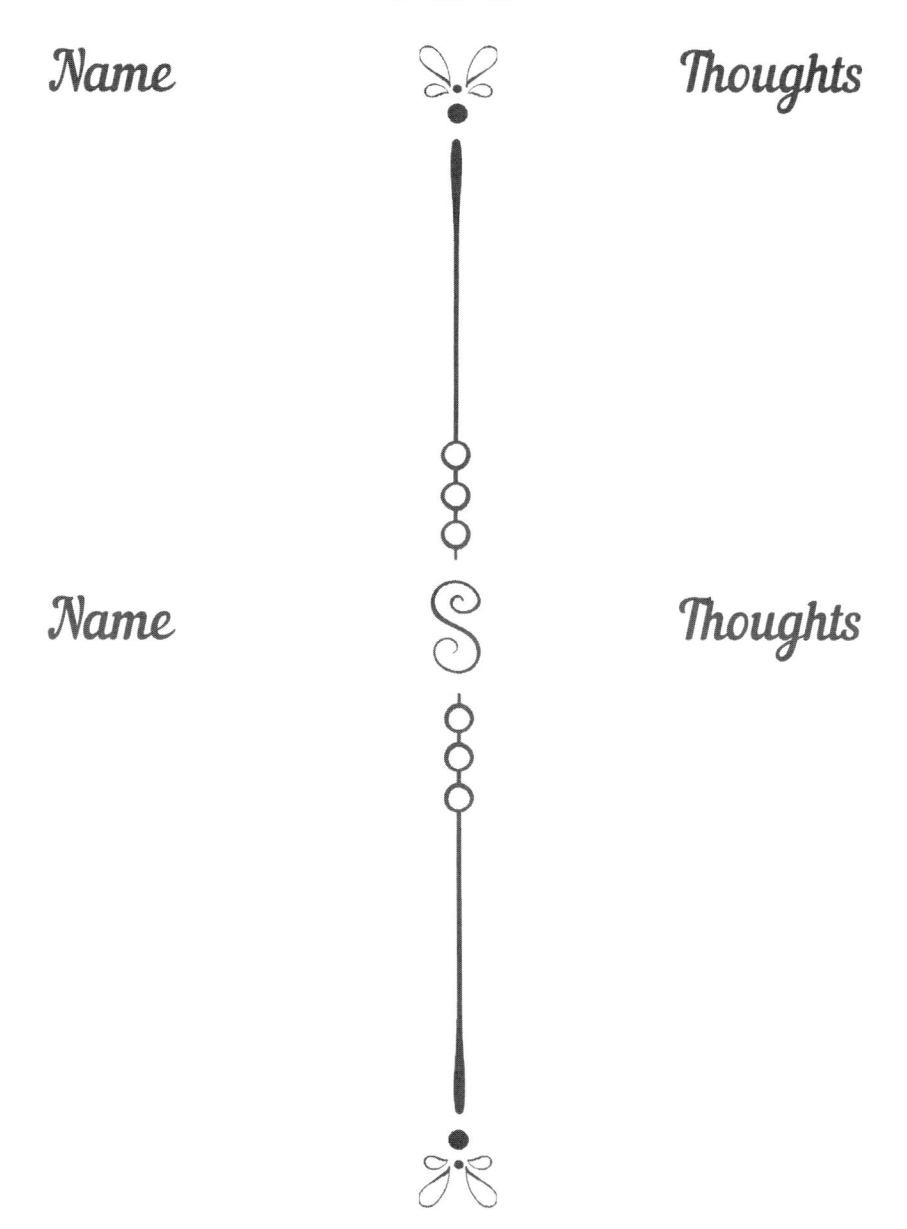

Printed in Great Britain
by Amazon